Financial Success for Teens

Easy to Learn Investing, Career Planning,
and Money Management Skills to Achieve
Early Financial Freedom

Sam Peterson

Introduction

Financial literacy might not sound like the most interesting thing, but let me assure you that it is not only important but essential for the rest of your life. You probably want to have enough money to live a great life when you are older. Let me tell you that all of this starts right now. When you are a teenager, that is the perfect time to start building up your financial success so that you do not have to struggle when you are older. If you speak to any adult, they will definitely tell you that they wish they would have started planning their finances way earlier than they actually did. This is because we tend to make a lot of mistakes with our finances in our earlier days. Mistakes can be easily avoided if the right guidance has been given. The goal of this book is to give you the right guidance so that you can step into your future financially prepared.

In this book, we are going to go over three major aspects of financial success. These are going to be investing, career planning, and money management. You need all of these things to be in place for you to build the type of future you want. Your finances will be in a much better place when you understand these principles and topics. This might sound super serious, but don't worry, we are going to have some fun along the way. I don't want this to just be a theoretical journey where you read through a bunch of information and not know how to implement it in your life. I want this to be something practical that you can take throughout your day and think about how you can implement what you have learned. There will be case studies and stories to help you fully understand the principles you are learning as well as exercises for you to complete to make sure you really understand the information you are reading.By the time you come to the end of this three-part book, you should be in a better financial place than you ever were before. Difficult financial concepts will become easier for you to understand, and you will be able to put a plan in motion for your finances. Whatever your goals are for your future, you can start planning and preparing for them right now. You don't have to wait until you're earning millions of dollars to start planning for your financial success. Let's get started so you can get yourself to financial success as soon as possible.

PART 1

Easy to Learn Investing

CHAPTER 1

Introduction to Investing

Have you ever thought about investing? What is the first thing that comes to your mind? Most teenagers don't really know much about investing, but this is the perfect time to start learning. You are in the perfect position because the younger you are, the more you can get out of investing. Even if you only have $2 in your piggy bank, you can still plan for the future and when you do have some money to spare, you will know exactly what to do with it. You are never too young to learn about investing or any other topics surrounding money.

Let's give you a rundown of what investing actually is. It's not the complicated topic you might think it is. When most adults speak about it, they can make it sound very intense, and that can be intimidating. This actually leads to a lot of adults not fully understanding investing, either. Instead of using all the fancy terms that can result in this confusion, we are going to learn about it in a way that is easy to comprehend. Then you will see that you can do it too.

Investing is an umbrella term. This means that there are many different types and ways that you can invest. Investing is simply putting your money in something that has the potential to give you even more money down the line. If you place $50 into a piggy bank or even a regular bank account, after a few months or years, you will still have that $50. Nothing will happen to it. This is saving your money. Saving is a good practice and can be thought of as the step before investing. If you choose to invest that $50, you could potentially have $100, $300, or even $1,000 in a few years. Investing allows you to grow your money.

So, why is investing important? There is this little thing called inflation. You have probably heard your parents, aunts, uncles, or grandparents speaking about how the price of certain things has increased since they were young. They could probably use $1 to buy a lot more stuff than we could years ago. This is due to inflation. The price of items increases slightly over time and that means the power of a dollar gets less as time passes. If you put your $50 into your piggy bank and leave it there for about 10 years, the value of the money will go down when you want to spend it. You will still have the same amount of money, but you will be able to buy fewer items. This is why investing is an important concept. You want your money to increase in value over time and not decrease.

Investing allows your money to grow faster than the rate of inflation and it will make you a lot wealthier in the long run. Investments will grow based on interest rates. This shows the rate at which your money will grow in a certain period of time. It is important to know the interest rate of the investments you plan to take out. There are so many different types of investments, but we are going to get into that in the next chapter.

Interest rate: The percentage rate your money will grow per predetermined time period.

The Power of Compound Interest

Gaining interest is the whole point of investing. Your money is growing without you doing anything. We have already mentioned interest rates and why this is so important, but did you know that there are two different types of interest? These are simple and compound interests. You may have learned about these in school, but just in case, let's do a quick recap.

Simple interest: The amount earned on the initial investment amount (Nickolas, 2022).

Here's the formula to work out simple interest:

Initial amount $\times$ annual interest rate $\times$ time period of loan in years $=$ Simple interest

So, let's say you wanted to invest $1,000 at an interest rate of 6% for 20 years.

$1,000 \times .06 \times 20 = $1,200

You would have gained $1,200 in interest leaving you with a total of $2,200 at the end of the 10 years. All you have to do is make sure the money stays in the investment account so you can gain this interest.

Compound interest: The interest is calculated based on the initial amount as well as the interest earned (Nickolas, 2022).

When you use compound interest your money grows faster because you are earning interest on interest. The longer you invest, the faster your money will grow. Here is the formula for compound interest:

Initial amount $\times$ (1 + annual interest rate)$^{(\text{time period in years})}$ - Initial amount $=$ Compound interest

Let's use the same figures from the simple interest equation so we can see the difference:

$$\$1,000 \times (1 + .06)^{20} - \$1,000 = \$2,207$$

Your total would be $3,207 as opposed to the $2,200 you had when you invested using simple interest. All that changed was the type of interest used, and it made a huge difference. You might be looking at this example and asking yourself how this would build wealth. I mean, $3,207 is a far cry from being rich and it took 20 years to get there. Before you lose hope in the system, take into account that this example is just used to show you the difference between the two interest types. In the real world, you would be depositing money into your investment accounts on a regular basis. This will speed up the whole process. Most investment accounts require a monthly deposit, so your money will continue to grow.

Now that we understand how compound interest works, it is also important to know how time impacts this. The sooner you invest, the more money you will have in your investment accounts. Many adults only wait until they are much older to start investing, and this results in them making a lot less money than they could have. Even a small amount invested over a long period of time will outperform a larger amount in a smaller amount of time.

We aren't going to do the calculations for this manually because the formulas can get a bit confusing. If you would like to use your own numbers to see how time impacts compound interest all you have to do is type in an *investment calculator* into your search engine and you will find one that will do all the hard work for you. All you have to do is plug in the right numbers.

Just to show you how time will impact the growth of your investments, let's use the same numbers we used in the other examples. Your initial investment is $1,000, but you have decided to deposit $200 every month in an account with an interest rate of 6%. Here is what you can expect:

After 10 years: Interest earned = $9,285.54 for a total of $34,285.54

After 20 years: Interest earned = $44,894.86 for a total of $93,894.86

After 30 years: Interest earned = $127,646.09 for a total of $200,646.09

After 40 years: Interest earned = $294,821.27 for a total of $391,821.27

After 50 years: Interest earned = $613,186.91 for a total of $734,186.91

Just look at how much the money increases after every decade. At the end of the 50 years, you would have only contributed about $120,000 and ended up with almost 7 times more money. As you get older, you will likely have more money to invest and that means your monthly contributions will probably increase. This means the amount of money you will have at the end is going to be much bigger. Compound interest is a very important concept when it comes to investing. You don't need to have a lot of money to start investing; it is just important that you start as soon as you can so you can get the most out of this principle.

Another Reason to Start Young

Investing can be complicated, especially if you are looking to get into the more nitty gritty side of it. Those who start as young as possible will have an advantage over their peers because they have more time to learn. All the investment advice in the world cannot be a replacement for what you will learn when you actually start doing it. If you are looking into medical school for your future, you might notice that there is a period where the students learn from their books and study materials, but they also need to take part in practicals and to work in a hospital for a certain number of hours before they can graduate. Why is this? While the theory is important because it provides a foundation, they would never be ready to deal with being a doctor unless they are actually involved in practically applying the knowledge they learned. The same goes for investing. It is important to learn all you can about it, but you also have to actually do it in order to get good at it.

There are very few investors who have never made an investment mistake. Even the most prominent investors who have made this their career will tell you they have stumbled a few times. The good news is they were able to learn from it and change their strategies in order to increase the amount they make in the long term. When you start investing, you will be able to see how all the information you are learning applies in the real world and you can try new things as you go along. If you are young and you make a mistake, you still have a lot of time to make up for it and it is probably not going to be that big a deal. If you are older and close to retirement when you make a mistake, this could spell disaster for your finances. This is not to say older people can't invest, it is just a bit harder for them to do so and they will have to be more conservative with their choices.

Chapter Questions

- Why do you think investing is important?

- How much do you think you can invest each month?

- Explain compound interest in one sentence.

CHAPTER 2

The Different Types of

Investments

Imagine going to the grocery store and you really want to buy a chocolate bar. When you walk in and find the correct aisle, you will be met with lots of choices. There are chocolates with nuts, raisins, toffee, caramel, and a whole lot of other things. Not to mention the different brands that all give you a different taste or flavor. It is up to you to make the right choice. Even though they are all chocolate, there will be some that will meet your needs and criteria better than others. This is the same with investments. There are a lot of different types of investments, and they can all be good, but there will be a few that are best for you.

Understanding the types of investments that are available to you is so important. This will allow you to make the best decision for your future. When you first start learning about investments, the choices might seem like they are overwhelming. In this chapter, we are going through the most important ones, so you have a good idea of your options. Feel free to talk to your parents about the different types of investments you are interested in. They might be able to offer some additional guidance.

It is important for you to do your own research when it comes to the types of investments you are considering. There are different service providers based on location and many other factors. You should look to get the best deal and the best performance. A simple internet search will allow you to see which companies are the most popular and why. It is best to choose a reputable investment company or a bank for your first investment, so you know that they have a track record and know how to handle their customers.

With all of that being said, let's dive into the different types of investments out there.

High-Yield Savings Account

The first type of investment we are talking about is a high-yield savings account. This is a very low-risk investment, so it is a great option to start off with. *High yield* just means that the interest on the account is higher than a normal savings account. When it comes to these types of accounts, you will likely have to lock in your money for a certain period of time. The longer you decide to lock in your money, the higher the interest rate will be. For it to be worth it, you will have to lock in your money for several years. If you want to withdraw any amount before the set time, you will be charged a fee. This fee can be quite large, so make sure you understand this before taking out this type of account.

A high-yield savings account is a great way for you to get into the habit of putting money away for the future. You will be able to plan and save without any risk. With this being said, there are many other investment types that have higher interest rates. If you put most of your money in a high-yield savings account, you will not see the full benefits of investing. Perhaps use this type of account until you decide where you want to invest for the long term, but this should not be the only investment type you have.

Stocks

You might have heard about the stock market before. There are many movies about it, *The Wolf of Wall Street* being one of the most popular. If you have ever watched the movie, you would know that you should not try to follow in the character's footsteps. However, the stock market does bring a lot of opportunities for investment. Before we start talking about why you should consider investing in stocks, you first need to understand what a stock is.

Stock: A representation of owning a set portion of a company or cooperation.

When you purchase a stock, you are essentially purchasing a part of the company it belongs to. Before you get too excited about owning part of the company, this is a very small portion of the company and doesn't mean you will have any decision power or can be part of the board meetings. How it works is the company will decide to sell a certain portion of the company on the stock market. This is divided into even smaller portions so that average people can invest in it. This allows the company to have access to additional funds so they can expand and grow their company. As the company grows, it will increase in value, and the value of each individual stock will increase. This is how you make money from the stock market.

The stock market can be confusing for beginners, so it is helpful to think of it like a marketplace. Have you ever been to a flea market or a farmers market? If so, you have probably walked past many stalls selling different items. Let this farmers market represent the stock market and each stall represents each company in the stock market. You are free to browse around and look at all the stalls before you make a decision. You can then go up to the stall and purchase a stock for a certain price. You have the freedom to decide how long you want to hold onto that stock before selling it again. During the time you have the stock in your possession, the price can increase or decrease. Once you are ready to sell, you will need to find someone who wants to buy it at its current value. If you sell it for more than you bought it for, you will make a profit.

The stock market is just a place for buyers and sellers to meet up and trade their stocks. It can be tempting to buy and sell quickly, but this is not usually the best strategy. For one, it is incredibly time-consuming. It is also really difficult to make a huge profit if you are constantly buying and selling. It typically takes time to see the true benefits of the stock market. You also have to remember that the stock prices will go up and down each day, month, and year. This can make people panic because nobody wants the price of their stock to decrease. Don't be discouraged because the overall trend of the stock market has been positive over long periods of time.

Let's look at the stock prices of some of the largest companies so you can get a better idea of the increase:

Company	Price in December 2010	Price in January 2023
Apple	$9.81	$143.00
Microsoft	$21.81	$242.71
Tesla	$17	$178

If your parents decided to invest $1,000 in Apple in 2010, they would have over $14,000 today. Not to mention that this is not the highest the stock prices have ever been. As you can see, there is a huge benefit to investing in the stock market. Most people will invest each month, so the amount they have invested keeps increasing. This results in them having even more investment capital.

Bonds

A bond is a lot less exciting than stocks, but it is lower risk and less complicated. Most people choose to have a mixture of stocks and bonds in their investment portfolios. This is to balance out the risk factor, so the investor can make the largest amount of money with a smaller amount of risk. Bonds are a great way to go if you are just starting out with investing because you will have a more stable investment for your money. However, the rate of return is going to be much lower than stocks. Let's define a bond:

Bond: A financial instrument that allows you to lend money to the government or a company for a set interest rate (Gobler, 2022).

When you buy a bond, you will be lending the money to the entity who issued the bond. Governments and companies do this, so they have more capital for growth and other endeavors. You will be signing a contract that states how long you will have to hold the bond and when that time is up, you will get your investment back plus the interest. Even though a bond is a safer investment option, there is still a chance for you to lose out. For example, if the company that issued the bond goes bankrupt, you might not be able to get your money back. This is typically not common, but it can happen.

Funds

Funds are a great way to invest when you are a beginner. You don't have to worry about most of the ins and outs of investing because you have someone handling it for you. The two most common funds are mutual funds and exchange-traded funds. With these funds, you will pay a certain amount each month to the company issuing the fund. Then your money will be pooled together with other investors. The fund manager will decide how the investments work, and you will continue to grow your money until the date you are able to take out the cash.

In most cases, the fund will have a mixture of stocks and bonds in it. This is to make sure each investor gets the most out of their investments with a lower amount of risk. You can also decide how you want your money to be used and whether you are willing to make riskier investments. It is important to talk to the consultant and ask as many questions as you can. This will help you fully understand what is happening with your money

If you are under the age of 18 or 21 (depending on the state you live in) you will not be able to open an account or fund on your own. This goes for many types of investments, not just funds. In this case, you should speak to your parents or guardians about opening a custodial account. The adult will have control over the account until you have turned 18 or 21. They will be making investments into the account on your behalf. After you turn the stipulated age, you will take full control of it and be able to do with it as you please. The parent or guardian does not own the money in the fund or account. It will still belong to you and cannot be used by them during the time you are still considered a minor. It's a great way to start investing at a young age. You can talk to your parents or guardian and work out how much you are willing to deposit into the account each month. Perhaps they would like to add something extra for you as well. It never hurts to ask!

Retirement Accounts

You are probably very far off from retirement at your young age! However, it is never too early to think about it. In fact, the earlier the better. The sooner you start investing in a retirement account, the more money you will have at that point in life. A retirement plan will have certain benefits, such as lower tax rates.

Tax: A compulsory levy that must be paid to the government based on your salary and yearly earnings (Gorton, 2021).

You probably don't pay any tax right now, but you might have heard a few adults complain about it. When you start earning a certain amount of money, you will be obligated to pay taxes to your country. The intended use of this money is to take care of the country. Everyone wants to pay as little tax as possible so they can keep more of their own money, so a retirement account is a great option.

IRAs and Roth IRAs are very common retirement accounts that can be opened by an individual person. A 401(k) is another retirement account, but this can only be opened through an employer. You will only be able to get this account if your employer offers it. It is a good idea to start looking into career paths that will allow you the opportunity to get a 401(k) as most employers will also match this contribution up to a certain amount—basically earning you free money! This means you will be able to invest a lot more and have a really good amount when you retire.

Real Estate

Real estate investing is when you invest in property. It is not likely that you will be able to do this right now, but you can plan for it, so you will have the opportunity to do so in the future. Real estate is a really solid investment, as it appreciates in value over time. This means that you will be able to sell your property for more than you bought it for.

There are plenty of ways you can invest in real estate. Some people purchase a property and fix it up a little in order to sell it for more shortly after. You could also purchase property and rent it out to others for a fee. This is a steady stream of income that can be made without much effort on your part. Even just purchasing a property to live in is an investment because if you ever want to sell, you will likely make a profit.

Other

There are tons of other investment types, and as you get more into investing you, can start considering them. We aren't going to go into much detail about these because they can be complicated, and you will need a large sum of money to start. These are not the type of investments most people start out with, so when you are older and ready, then you can see if this is something you want to try. Here is a list of a few of them:

- Annuities

- Derivatives

- Precious Metals

- Energy (Oil, Coal, Etc.)

- Artwork

Chapter Questions

- What investment type was the most interesting to you?

- Discuss what a stock is in one sentence.

- How much do you think you can invest each month?

CHAPTER 3

How to Create an Investment Plan

The first step to investing is having a plan. Unfortunately, this is also the most boring step! Most teenagers don't like to sit down and create a plan. I get it, it is way more fun to just dive in. However, when it comes to your money, do you really want to jump in and hope for the best? As tempting as it might be to skip the planning stage, it is the part of the process that will make everything else a whole lot easier for you. Don't worry, you don't have to know everything just yet. All you need to do is create some sort of blueprint for yourself so you can track your investments. This will help you make better choices moving forward and you will be able to see how your money is growing.

What Do Your Finances Look Like?

Before you start developing your plan, you need to know your starting point. Have a look at your finances and think about how to plan for investing. This might mean putting away some of your pocket money and not spending it on that new pair of sneakers or buying a soda every day at school. Investing often takes some sacrifice because you must see where your priorities lie. You will be thankful you did when you have set yourself up for your financial future.

The best way to look at your finances is to create a budget for yourself. It is actually pretty easy to do this. All you need to figure out is how much you make each month and subtract your expenses. It is best to create columns for this so you can easily see where your money goes. Here's an example of what your budget might look like:

Budget for the Month

Income:

	Expected income	Actual income
Monthly allowance	$60	$60
Earnings for mowing the	$20	$20 + $5 tip

neighbor's lawn		
Earnings from washing cars	$30	$30
Gift from Grandparents	$30	$30
Total	$140	$145

Expenses:

	Planned expenses	**Actual expenses**	**Leftover**
Investments	$40	$40	$0
Saving for new sneakers	$30	$30	$0
Mother's Day	$15	$13	$2

present			
Snacks	$20	$15	$5
Going out with friends	$35	$34	$1
Total	$140	$132	$8 + $5 = $13

You can use the above example to work out your own budget. You can see in the sample budget, there is $13 leftover. If this happens to you, feel free to allocate it wherever you want to. Perhaps you can put it toward saving for something you want, or you can add some extra into your investments. The main thing is that you do not go over your budget and end up spending more than expected. This will lead to you having to take away money from your savings and investments. Do your best to stick to the budget so you can get the most out of your money.

Think About Your Goals

If you want to invest successfully, you will need to know why you are investing in the first place. You might be thinking, *I just want to be rich!* Well, that's a great starting point, but let's get more specific. Think about what you want to do with the money once you have saved up enough. Perhaps you want to be able to buy a car by the time you start college or maybe you want to start saving up for college, so you don't have to take out huge student loans. You can ask your parents or guardians for help with this if you cannot decide. They might be able to give you insight into what you will need in the coming years.

The reason your goals are so important is that it will help keep you motivated. If you don't know what you are saving toward, what's the point of saving? You will find it a lot more tempting to spend your money on things now, than to save and invest for the future. Your goals also give you a good idea of how much you actually need to save. If you are saving up for a new car, you can research your options and get a general idea of how much you will need in the next few years. From here, you will be able to decide how much you will need to save each month in order to get to your goal. This helps you to be realistic with your investing goals and create a plan that allows you to get what you want.

Decide What You Want to Invest In

In the previous chapter, we spoke about all the different types of investments out there. From this, you probably have a few that stick out to you. Do some additional research on these and see how you can get into investing in these areas. Different countries and states have different laws that govern them, so you will need to make sure that you actually can invest in those areas. The easiest way to do this is to do a quick internet search and see if any popular banks and financial service providers have these products available.

Open Up a Dummy or Mock Portfolio

Investing in stocks and funds can seem confusing and many people are hesitant because they do not know what to expect. If you find yourself in this position, I have some good news. You can open up a "fake" investing portfolio that mimics the real thing. You don't have to invest any real money, but you will get a good idea of how investing works. These are called dummy or mock portfolios.

A few options are Mockportfolio.com and Wall Street Survivor. There are also many stockbrokers who will allow you to run a free trial for a short period before you commit to them. This will allow you to see what the broker provides, and you will get the lay of the land before you have to put down any money. These are really good options, and because there is no financial commitment, it will seem a lot less daunting.

Start Investing

Now that you have done all the legwork, you can start investing. It might take you a few months to get to this point, and that is perfectly normal. In some cases, you will have to save up a larger sum of money in order to get started. You can take this time to learn from your dummy portfolio so that you are fully prepared. Then you can put some real money in the game.

This can be really exciting but remember to not get carried away. Stick to the plan you made and allow your investing to work on its own. Remember to be consistent because this is the best way to grow your money. You can make changes to your investment strategy as you go along but it is much easier to do this once you have actually started. Investing and saving should be the first places your money goes at the start of the week or month. This is a great habit to get into and it will serve you well as you get older.

Keep Track of Your Portfolio

It is important to keep track of what you are investing in. Things can change very quickly, so if you keep track of your investments, you will be able to see what is working and what isn't. Leaving your investments to their own devices means that you might not pick up on a problem early enough to do something about it. This can lead to losses, and it is never fun when that happens.

You don't have to check on your investments every day. In fact, that is not advisable. Checking on this every few weeks should be good enough to understand what is going on. You might realize that one of your investments is doing poorly and perhaps you need to take your money out and place it in another stock or type of investment. This is pretty normal when you are an investor.

When you keep track, make sure you are making notes about each investment. This will help you recognize patterns, and this is valuable information throughout your investment journey. Even though the advice of other investors can be useful, it is usually better to make your own choices based on your experience and knowledge.

Chapter Questions

- How much money do you have to spare for investing?

- What goals do you have for your money?

- List out the dummy, or mock, investing sites that you could sign up for along with the pros and cons of each.

CHAPTER 4

Tips for Successful Investing

It is always helpful to have a few tips and tricks to help you through investing. Even though making mistakes is one of the best ways to learn, you don't want to make unnecessary ones. You will definitely make a few bad calls at some point, but if you can limit your setbacks, that will always be the best way to go.

Make It a Habit

Back when I was in school, many moons ago, there was this kid named Craig. This guy used to go to the gym every day after school, but if you asked me, I could never tell the difference between him and every other boy in my class. He was of a very normal build, in my opinion. One day we were paired together in science class, and we got along quite well. I basically flat out asked him why he wasted his time after school going to the gym when he could be enjoying some down time or hanging out with the rest of us. He simply said, "It's just a habit, I guess." Even though I could not understand why you would give up an hour a day to get all sweaty at the gym, I left it.

At the end of the school year, we had an annual pool party at one of the rich kids' houses. Everyone was invited, and it was a chance for the guys to impress the girls with their mad backflipping skills. Craig was there and, as one does at a pool party; he took his shirt off. Which revealed some chiseled abs and defined biceps that put every other guy to shame. That day, Craig got the most female attention of any guy in the school. I just remember thinking that if this is the result of a habit, then I need to change the way I do things.

I know what you are thinking: *What does this have to do with investing?* I'm getting there. You see, Craig made going to the gym a priority in his life even when all of us were hanging out and goofing off. We thought it was a waste of time and energy because he didn't look much different from any of us. He just kept going and built a habit that allowed him to slowly make changes to his body, and one day, he was able to see the true benefits of this and it put all of us to shame. When it comes to creating habits with your money, other people might not understand why you are choosing not to go out every weekend or why you have decided to pick up some extra work to increase your income. These things will not make sense because there is no immediate gratification, but one day, things will change. You will notice how far you have come and then it will make sense to the people around you. Building a habit keeps you consistent even when you might not feel motivated because you aren't progressing as fast as you would like. It will become like second nature, and you will eventually reap the benefits.

Don't Let Emotions Take Over

Emotions and financial decisions should not be in the same field. Emotions will almost always override any logical thought, so you need to put them on the bench when you are playing any kind of financial game. I often hear people talk about how they are not emotional. If you are one of those people, I have some unfortunate news for you. We are all emotional, whether we acknowledge it or not. Emotions are not a bad thing, but they can lead to some bad decisions.

Let's take the stock market, for example. This is one of the most volatile investments, even though it has a track record of bringing the best returns. One day, you could make major gains and increase your investment capital and the next, the market could take a dive and you will end up with less than you started with. In this case, many people scramble and remove their money from the stock market, so their losses aren't as big. This decision is fueled by fear, anxiety, or some other negative emotion. Since the market often jumps back up again, it would be a bad choice to pull out of the market based on these emotions. You would have a better chance of increasing your investments if you kept your money in the stock market and waited for the down period to pass. This means putting your emotions aside and sticking to your original plan.

If you have a plan or blueprint for how you want to invest, try to stick to it as closely as you can. There is no reason to jump around and make changes on the spot. If you have done your research and are happy with your choices, then leave it at that. You can schedule check-ins with yourself to see how your investments are performing. This is a good time to re-evaluate if need be. When things are structured, it will help keep those pesky emotions in check.

Expect Some Losses

Here's the thing about investing, it's not always going to go your way. This is especially so when you are talking about the stock market. This and many other investments tend to be quite volatile. This means they go up and down all the time. Since you cannot fully predict what is going to happen there might come a time where you lose out. This doesn't mean that you lose all your money but that you don't make the kind of increases you hoped for. This is completely normal, and the longer you are investing for, the more you will understand how this works. If you do hit a point in your investment journey where you experience some losses, don't get too discouraged. You have time; since you have started investing earlier; it is not too big of a deal. Take it as a learning opportunity so you can get better in the future.

Research Your Investments

This is especially important when you are investing in the stock market and in companies. Different companies and sectors of companies will perform at different levels depending on what is going on in the economy. A sector is like a group or class that forms part of the economy. For example, Apple and Microsoft will fall under the technology sector while Berkshire Hathaway and J.P. Morgan Chase will be under the finance sector. There are certain events that will impact how each sector performs. There might also be something happening within a certain company that leads to their stocks declining in price.

There are a lot of factors to take into consideration when you are researching your investment. It is usually best to invest in a company that you know a little bit about and are interested in. This way it is not going to be as big of a burden to do your research and keep up-to-date with what is going on with that company. Restructuring of employees or leaders, bad financial decisions, and a general market downturn can impact the price of stocks. If you keep up-to-date with the news, then you will be able to get ahead of what might happen to your investments and make a better decision before you are stuck. In most cases, it is best to leave your investments as is, but there might be a time when you have to take your money out to prevent further losses.

Chapter Questions

- How do you plan on making investing a habit?

- Are you an emotional person when it comes to money? How can you prevent emotions from getting in the way?

- What investments are you most interested in and why?

CHAPTER 5

Let's Get Practical

It is all well and good to have theoretical knowledge, but you also have to put it into practice. When it comes to investing, you will need to actually do it in order to get good at it. In this chapter, we are going to be discussing a few practical things you can do to prepare you for investing and to help get the ball rolling. You will notice that many of these have been discussed in previous chapters, so you should be able to start applying them. If you are confused about anything, you can go back to the relevant chapter and find some guidance.

Put More Into Investing

In order to invest more, you might need to increase how much you earn. There are plenty of ways to make some extra money as a teenager. Here are some ideas to help you think:

- Ask your parents for more responsibility at home for additional allowance money.

- Look for a part-time job around town.

- Make something and sell it.

- Offer to do tasks for your neighbors like walk their dogs, babysit, or mow their lawn.

- When summer rolls around, find a summer job.

There will be many opportunities to make money if you look for it. Remember not to take on more than you can handle, because you don't want school and your personal life to suffer for it. The goal is to allow yourself the opportunity to increase your earnings, but ensure you are being realistic about what you can handle.

It is a good idea to make your own list of potential ways you can make some extra money. You can use the template below to help decide which options will be best suited for you. Depending on your skills, spare time, lifestyle, and city, your options will differ. It's all about being resourceful.

Potential income source	Expected income	Time needed

Research Potential Stocks

Take some time to research a few stocks you are interested in. It helps to see what is going on with the stocks and whether they are very stable, volatile, declining, or increasing in price. You will be able to make better investment decisions this way. You can use the template below to help you do this or you can create your own.

Company name	Average price 2 years ago	Average price this month	Notes

PART 2

Career Planning

CHAPTER 6

Introduction to Career Planning

When I was five years old, I knew exactly what I wanted to be when I grew up. I wanted to sail around the world and be a pirate! I watched a lot of movies and shows about pirates and how they explored the seven seas. I was quite adamant about it and my parents definitely did play along. However, fast forward a few decades, and my feelings about being a pirate have definitely changed. In fact, my body completely rejects the idea of sailing around on the ocean for months on end. I actually have severe seasickness, so even if this was something I wanted to do, it's definitely not going to be practical.

What did you want to be when you were younger? As kids, we have these lofty ideas of these amazing jobs or careers that look so fun and captivating. This is also fueled by what we see on TV. Most of these things are not really realistic. Becoming a pirate, astronaut, princess, or lion tamer might all sound amazing and filled with adventure, but most of us will never be those things. In today's world, there are certain jobs that will provide a steady income and others that will leave you struggling. You might have had these kinds of ideas of what you're going to become when you're older, but it is important to be realistic so that you can make smart choices for your own future. This doesn't mean that you have to do something boring or something that you hate, it just means you have a better plan and understand what your potential future could look like. I, for one, am glad I didn't go to pirate school!

There are a few things that you need to know when you are career planning and we're going to be going through them in the chapter. This will help you to understand what career planning is before we get to the meat of this part of the book.

Who Are You?

The first thing you need to find out is who you are and what kind of person you are. Every person is completely different, and this means they have different strengths and weaknesses. If you want to choose a fulfilling career, then you will need to choose something that is in line with your strengths and interests. People who truly enjoy what they are doing are the ones that excel because it's easier to propel yourself forward with something you truly enjoy than with something you struggle with.

In many cases, this is actually the hardest part of your career planning because truly knowing who you are at a young age can be very confusing. As you grow, you will most likely change in various areas and it's okay to allow yourself to do that. With that being said, there are clues to who you are now that can show you what your potential future could be later on. You probably have a few likes and interests that play a big part in your life. Perhaps you are somebody who truly enjoys math and is very good at it, or maybe you are a sportsperson and enjoy being outdoors. You could be somebody who enjoys research and finding out new things or somebody that enjoys playing around with technology. All of these things could lead you down a specific career path if you explore them a little.

What Is Out There?

The next thing you're going to need to do when you are career planning is to figure out what kind of careers and jobs are out there. If I stuck to my dreams of being a pirate, it was going to be a very difficult journey for me. Believe it or not, there isn't that much demand for pirates these days. There might be things that you are passionate about and that interest you, but there simply isn't a market for it. In this case, you should be looking for other avenues to enjoy your specific interest while following another career path. Sometimes our passions need to be funded by a more stable career and this will allow us to enjoy the things we are passionate about, but in a more realistic way.

What Do You Need to Do?

Once you have thought about what your skills and talents are and what availability there is for jobs and careers in this area, you need to start thinking about what you need to do in order to get there. Some careers require you to study for a long period of time so you can get the relevant qualifications in order to practice your skills. Other career paths will allow you to jump in and get started straight out of school. You need to have a look at what will get you to your ultimate goal. Taking some time to research how people have gotten into the positions they are in now is going to be crucial for you. You can follow in their footsteps, and it will make the journey a lot easier for you because you know exactly what you need to do. This will also allow you to prepare your parents in advance just in case they need to help fund your studies or skills development. It will help you to put a plan in place and give you a realistic idea of how long it will take you to get to your ultimate goal.

Now that we have discussed exactly how you plan for your career, we are going to dig a little deeper to help you develop a solid plan. This is an incredibly valuable part of planning your future and becoming financially successful. Doing this as early as possible in your life is essential and you will definitely thank yourself in the future.

CHAPTER 7

Assessing Your Strengths and Interests

In the previous chapter, we spoke about getting to know who you are and asserting your strengths and weaknesses is a big part of this. There are many different aspects to your strengths and weaknesses that you should evaluate in order to better plan for your future career. It is very important that you are realistic with this as it can be very easy to overestimate what we're good at. It might also be a good idea to speak to people who are close to you and get their input on what they think you are good at and where your strengths lie. You might actually be surprised at the feedback you get, but take it in your stride as all this information is very valuable.

There are four main categories that you need to look at in order to assess your strengths and your interests. This is going to be incredibly helpful as you move through the journey of planning in your career and your future. Take some time to really think about each area and give yourself some honest feedback. You might not be able to do all of this in one day, so it is okay to take a break and come back a few days later and see if you have different answers.

Skills and Talents

Your skills and talents are the things you are inherently good at. You might notice in school that people tend to separate based on their skills or talents. Kids that are good with a musical instrument or can sing tend to join music classes or be part of theater groups. Kids who are very academic and always get good grades stick together and might even be part of an academic group or advanced class in the school. Those who are more athletic will be found on the sports field. There are many other skills and talents that have not been mentioned that you might exhibit and see at your school or around you.

Take some time to look at the things that you are naturally good at. You can look back to when you were a child and see what you gravitated toward. You could also ask your parents, guardians, or siblings for some input here. Tell them that you want them to be honest so that you understand yourself better.

Sometimes, older people will tell us a lie just to not hurt our feelings, but that isn't really helpful when we are trying to figure out what we want to do with our lives.

If you are really confused about what your skills and talents are, it is a perfect time to start trying new things. I am usually surprised at how many times people have secret skills and talents that they never knew about. If you never try, then you will never know. That is why myself, and so many of my friends, have implemented a monthly "try something new" rule. Each month, we have to try one new thing. This could be something big or small. There are also no rules as to what these things have to be. The main goal is to get into the habit of trying something new.

There will be some months where I will end up trying out something quite big, like visiting a new country or signing up for a new club or sport. Other times, it will be something small, like trying a new type of food, learning a new recipe, going to a part of town I never have, or writing on a new topic. Not everything is skill and talent related, but it helps me get to know myself better. I create space in my life for new things and it makes it easier for me to find the things that I am good at and that bring me joy. I have met so many new people and had amazing experiences through doing this, and I am sure you will as well.

Make a list of skills and talents you think you might be good at and once you have given it a shot, rate yourself out of ten. This way, you will be able to see what skills and talents you have that you might not have known before.

Skill	Description	Rating
		/10
		/10
		/10
		/10

Values and Goals

Your values and goals are going to form a huge part in your career path. We are not all made the same and that means there are certain career paths and companies that are not going to sit well with us. I remember one of the jobs I had in my early career. I was working as an assistant for the manager at a large company. I actually enjoyed the work, but the culture of the company was not right for me. People used to be very disrespectful to each other in meetings. What was just supposed to be a weekly report would turn into screaming matches. Even though I did not contribute much to these meetings, I ended up leaving the room feeling so drained and despondent. There were some people who worked there who didn't mind this because they said it was a way to get all their frustration out and it wasn't necessarily held against them, but it really wasn't for me.

I realized that if I wanted to climb up the ladder in that company, I would have to become like them. I didn't feel all too comfortable with that, so I left. My values didn't align with theirs, so it was best for me to bow out and find a place that did match my values and would allow me to reach my career goals in a healthier way. As you get on the career journey, you might find yourself in a company, or sector, that is not aligned with your goals or values. It is your job to assess this and decide how you want to move forward. If you have already established your goals and values, then it will be a lot easier for you to pick the right jobs and career paths. You can tell a lot about a company and its culture when you are in the interview and through research. Many companies will post their goals and values on their website, so it is free information for you to check out. You will likely notice that many companies in the same sector will have similar goals and values, so this is helpful when you are choosing a career path.

There are many things that can play into your goals and values. For example, if you want to be a CEO of a large corporation one day, then you would have to do your best to walk a path that can lead you to that. You will need to look at the skills required of a leader in this setting and start developing those skills. You will likely need to study something in business or tech in order to get into one of these companies, so you can build up your career. If you are someone who is not looking to be stuck in an office for most of the day, you will have to pick a career that aligns with that. Something that will allow you to be out in nature or even something in sales or consulting where you will be out and about seeing customers and clients. There are so many different career paths out there and it can all seem confusing and overwhelming. Listing out your goals and values will allow you to narrow down your options and make it more manageable.

Your Interests

Your interests could play a huge part in your career path in many different ways. Some people will get a job that aligns with their interests and others will get one that will help fund their interests. Let me explain. Jason is a friend I knew from college. He has always been interested in fishing. He was the type of guy to plan 5 a.m. fishing trips, of which I only went on one because at 5 a.m., my 19-year-old brain was not functioning at full steam. This was something he was truly interested in, and he knew a lot about it. I swear, if he could live on a boat on the lake, he would be so happy.

I always thought he would go into something related to fish or the ocean. Perhaps become a marine biologist or a fishmonger. To my surprise, he was studying computer programming at college and to me, it didn't make any sense. He didn't strike me as the computer nerd type of person. He was definitely more of a fish nerd type of person. Anyway, when he graduated, he got a job at a good company and worked there for a few years before he decided to open his own business. His business took off, and he is now able to work from wherever he wants to and make a living. Can anyone guess where his workplace of choice is? If you guessed on a boat in the lake, you would be right! He bought a great leisure boat that allows him to sit out on the lake and fish in style. He can do it whenever he wants, and this allows him to fulfill his passions and interests without it actually being his job.

I met up with him for coffee not too long ago and we chatted about our time in college and where we ended up in life. I had to tell him that I was quite surprised that he didn't choose a job that had something to do with water or fish, since that is clearly what he is interested in. He explained that he was glad he didn't because then he would not have been able to fund his current lifestyle. Turning fishing into a job would have likely made him lose his passion for it and it would not have allowed him to have the time to spend with his family. He donates to a few charities that deal with ocean and lake clean ups and even volunteers with them a couple times a month.

Jason is good at his job, and he actually enjoys it even though it is not his number one passion. Sometimes we can believe the misconception that our passions should fuel our careers, but that is not always the case. Most people who are accountants are not so passionate about numbers and figures that they get excited when they have to audit someone's taxes. They are good with numbers and can use the money they earn to fund their passions and interests. If you are passionate about animals, you don't have to become a zookeeper. You can choose another career path that will allow you to fund vacations to see animals around the world and will give you the resources to donate to the right causes. Sometimes our passions and interests can feel like a box that we are stuck in, but it does not have to be that way. There are many ways you can choose to use your interests and passions to help decide on which career path to go on.

Chapter Questions

- What are you passionate about?

- Are there jobs in that field that will allow you to make a sustainable living?

- If not, what other careers could help fund your passions and interests?

Chapter 8

How to Research and Choose a Career Path

I remember being in school and thinking there were only a few careers to choose from. I mean, when we watched TV or listened to what our parents wanted us to be, the same few options kept popping up. Doctor, lawyer, and accountant were by far the most common ones. Then when I started looking into colleges and seeing how many degree options there were, I was quite surprised at the variety. I was even more surprised when I started researching different career paths and I noticed that there are so many to choose from that may not be talked about all too much.

When you get into the workforce your entire view of the working world is going to change. You will notice how many different paths there are that you might not have been exposed to. On top of that, the workforce is always changing. Right now,

I believe that we are in the middle of such a change. AI is on the scene, and it is making waves in the workforce. People are looking for new ways to utilize this technology to help their companies and businesses grow. This means that many jobs will shift and change to accommodate this. Half of the world is freaking out about this, and the other half is looking forward to what might happen. Back in the '90s the height of technology was the fact that everyone could have a corded phone in their homes. If you have ever watched the show *F.R.I.E.N.D.S*, then you would know what I am talking about. None of the characters had their own phones and now the world has completely shifted and changed. People have adapted and brand-new careers and job opportunities have come out to match the advancements made.

You don't have to have it all figured out right now, but you can set yourself up in the right direction. That is the point of career planning. You want to give yourself the best start. You might not know exactly where you will end up in 20 or 30 years, but you should have some sort of plan in place so that you don't have to be floating around for the foreseeable future.

Make a List and Start Searching

You probably have some idea of the careers out there. Perhaps you have done some research on the types of jobs people can do with a certain skill set you have. Make a list of all the potential careers you have in mind. As you move through the rest of this chapter, you will be adding and taking away some options on the list. The main point of having this list is to allow yourself to easily see all the options. You can make this list on your phone, laptop, or using good old-fashioned pen and paper.

Give yourself some space on the list to write a little bit about the career as well as some pros and cons. This will help you to know your options at a glance. It will also allow you to have some structure for your research. There are some fantastic resources out there that can help you get a better idea of what it is like to work in certain fields. Do a quick internet search of the careers you are interested in and see what pops up. You can also go onto YouTube and search "day in the life of xyz." Many people show what it is like working in their job roles, so you can get a better idea of what they do and how they spend their time. I would caution you by saying that many of these videos are the highlights of their jobs and not all the boring or really challenging stuff. It will help you get a general idea, but it might not always be accurate, so take it with a pinch of salt.

You can use this template for your list:

Job	Pros	Cons

Start Looking at Job Postings

Job postings give you a very realistic idea of what is out there and what companies are looking for. You will be able to see how many available jobs there are for certain careers. Something that is very specialized might not show up as much and might make it more difficult to break into the industry. If you are unsure about what you want to do in the future, it is usually best to pick a career path that is broader and will offer you more opportunities.

There are many job board websites that will allow you to filter jobs based on various criteria. These are incredibly helpful as you are doing your research. Try looking at a few different postings for similar job titles. This will give you a better idea of what is expected from someone stepping into that role. You will notice that different companies will require slightly different things from their employees. You shouldn't worry too much about the things that aren't skills or education. Company culture does change from company to company. This means that there will be some companies you will be the perfect fit for and others that don't align with your personality and values. Instead, focus on the things that you can build up.

Do Some Quizzes to Find Out More About Yourself

A fun way to get to know yourself and what career you might be suited for is to do some career quizzes. No, I am not talking about the quizzes where you pick your breakfast items, and it shows you what you should be doing with the rest of your life. While those quizzes can be fun, they are definitely not accurate. I'm looking at you, Buzzfeed! The quizzes and tests I am talking about are the ones that are made by professionals to get a better look at who you are as a person and then show you where your skills might be best used. I am going to put a quick disclaimer here: these are not always accurate and should not be taken as law. They are designed to help you narrow down what careers might be best suited for you, but that doesn't mean there aren't other options for you. The goal here is to open your eyes to careers you might not have thought about before.

As humans, we are all really bad at pinpointing our personality types. What you think you are like might not be reflective of what other people think of you. Doing a personality test is a great way to get a good idea of your personality and the key traits you exhibit. You will also get to know yourself a whole lot better and hopefully be able to choose your career path more clearly. There are tons of free personality tests that you can do online.

Some are longer than others, so you might need to carve out a good chunk of time in order to do them. I would suggest doing more than one so you can get a better idea of who you are. You will notice patterns emerging and that's when you know you definitely are a certain type of way and exhibit certain characteristics.

Many of these personality tests will give you a few examples of jobs you might be good at and that can be really helpful. You can cross-reference this to your career tests and see if there is any overlap. This whole process is going to help you understand yourself better and you might also be exposed to some career options you never knew about before. You can add these to the list you made at the beginning of this chapter. You might also want to remove a few career options now that you have a better understanding of yourself and what you might be good at.

Think About Salary

Potential salary is a really important thing to consider when you are planning out your career. Many teens don't think too hard about this because they are more focused on their passions and what they think they will enjoy. This is not wrong, but your salary will impact the type of life you will be able to live.

Someone who wants a more luxurious life will not be able to get by with minimum wage. Another person who is looking to live a simple life might not be happy with a high-paying corporate job. It really is important to think about the type of life you want and how much you will need in order to have that.

Career Days

Career days are a great way to expose yourself to various careers. There will be career days at schools and colleges, so even if your school doesn't have one, you will be able to find one somewhere. Attending a career day is simply allowing yourself to see what kind of careers are out there. You are also able to form connections with staffing and recruitment people who work for various companies. Many companies are always on the hunt for new talent and if you know what they are looking for, you will be able to tailor your resume to this when the time comes. Connections are really important when it comes to stepping into the career of your dreams. This is typically referred to as networking, and many adults will do it in order to meet people who can be beneficial to them in the future. You are far more likely to get hired if you have a relationship with someone in the company than if you simply applied online. There are also many job postings that are never posted online and are instead filled internally or through referrals. You increase your chances of getting the job of your dreams if you have more connections.

If you do find a career day close to where you live, take some time to explore it. Look into careers that you never thought you would be interested in because you will have access to more information. You can feel free to speak to the people who are manning the booths, as they will likely have some experience in the career you are looking into. There will also be pamphlets that you can take and read at home. This will give you even more information and will help you to make your decision when the time comes to choose your career.

Chapter Questions and Tasks

- Look through at least 10 different job postings for similar jobs and career paths.

- What stands out to you from your research?

- Based on your personality, what jobs suit you?

CHAPTER 9

Tips for Successful Career Planning

Career planning is something you are likely going to be doing a few times throughout your life. Understanding how to go about it and gaining as much information as possible is going to be essential. This will help the process go a lot smoother and will help you to get the best results in the end. You don't have to have everything figured out just yet, but setting yourself up for success is important.

Speak to Adults in the Careers You Want

If you are interested in a particular career, speak to an adult who already is in it. They will be able to tell you a lot of things that you might not be able to find out on the internet or through other means of research. They have first-hand experience in the job that you are looking at for your future. You'll be able to have a one-on-one conversation with them and it will make the career planning process a lot easier for you. Ask them how they got to where they are now and what advice they have for somebody wanting to walk the same path. Having these kinds of conversations will give you valuable information and it will help you to grow your professional network. Adults love it when teenagers are ambitious and want to learn more. They will definitely remember this later on if there is a specific role that needs to be filled.

You can ask your parents, grandparents, aunts, uncles, or any other adult to help find somebody who is in the career that you want to be in. They will be able to set up a meeting date so you can have a conversation with that person. Make sure you come with a list of questions and do your research beforehand so that you don't waste your time asking questions that could easily be answered through a bit of internet searching. This one-on-one meeting is supposed to get you some information that would be difficult to find.

When you have a meeting or phone call with the person, make sure that you are professional and polite. You never know whether this is going to be the first step on your career journey, and you want to make a good impression. If you have gone out to eat, then offer to pay the bill, as this leaves a good impression.

You don't have to take the person out for a five-course dinner; a simple coffee should be more than enough. It's all about making the effort to make the other person feel comfortable, so they open up and are willing to talk about whatever you want to. When you make this kind of effort, adults are more willing to share information with you and help you out throughout your journey. This is a good tip to take into your adult life, as you will continue networking for the foreseeable future. If you remain friendly and ensure that you are making an effort, you will see the benefits of this.

Look Into Things You Haven't Thought of Before

There are literally thousands of careers out there that could be a good fit for you. Limiting yourself to the options that you already have in mind can be a big mistake. Take some time to look into a few things that you have never thought of before. We tend to stick to our comfort zones because it requires less effort from us, but these are not always fulfilling in the long run. For example, you might be really good at math and think that accounting is a great career move for your future. While this may be true, you haven't actually taken the time to consider what else is out there. Maybe you have another skill or talent that could make a better career opportunity. Perhaps you enjoy public speaking or teaching other people. These could lead to a different career path that would make you a lot happier in the future.

While you are still young, it is important to explore as much as possible. You are allowed to make a few mistakes as you walk through life. Even if adults don't want to admit it, we have all made a few mistakes and those mistakes are what have led us to where we are now. You should never be afraid of trying something new or even failing. These things are simply part of life and the sooner you get comfortable with it, the better it is going to be for you. Always take the time to research things that are slightly different from what you might have had in mind. This will stretch your thinking and allow you to be a lot more open-minded as you start making decisions for your future career.

Look Into the Future

There are some career paths or industries that are declining and others that are growing. This is the normal progression of life, but it is important to pick a career that will be there for the next 50 years. This will allow you to have job security and you will have a better chance of finding a company that fits your goals and lifestyle. About 100 years ago, many people were factory workers. They would spend their days working on the factory floors in order to produce various goods. These days, there are still people needed on the factory floors, but the jobs are much different. We have machines that do the bulk of the work for us, and we need people to oversee production and make sure the machines are performing well. Someone who only knew how to be a factory worker would have a very hard time changing careers once the machines were introduced. A factory worker is not a future-proof job.

It is very likely that most jobs will change in some fashion in the future. However, you need to make sure the type of career or sector you are planning on working for will lead to a long-term career. Look into sectors that are on the rise so that you can see your options. Some of the options are:

- Nurses

- Technicians

- Data Scientists

- Research Analysts

- Athletic Trainers

These are just a few of the job roles that people are looking to fill. Do some research and see what other ones are out there. If you study something that is in demand, you will have a much easier time finding a job and leveraging your skills throughout your career.

Chapter 10

Case Studies and Exercises to Practice Career Planning

Taking some time to practice career planning skills is really important. In this chapter, we are going to be going through a few essential skills that you will need in order to plan your career and land the jobs you want. These can be used in your everyday life and not just be saved for the future. If you are looking for a part time job or something to do in the summer, you can think of it as the first step in your career.

Create Your First Resume

Creating a resume is a skill that you will need throughout your life. Whenever you apply for a new job, you will need this to show off your skills. Most people will have at least a few different jobs or want to move companies a few times throughout their career. Having this on hand is very helpful and it will allow you to sell yourself. Even if you are just applying for a summer job or part-time work, it is a good idea to have a well-constructed resume.

Once you have your resume, you will just need to add the relevant material as you go along. It becomes much easier this way. I would highly suggest that you always keep your resume up-to-date because you never know when you are going to need it. On top of that, it can get very difficult to remember everything you have done if you only look at it every few years.

Creating a resume also helps you to feel proud of your accomplishments and see how far you have come. It is a great way to make yourself feel proud of what you have done. Even as a young student you have probably done more than you think. Even if your resume looks really empty now, this is a chance for you to beef it up. See what you can do that would add something to the resume. Maybe work a bit harder to get better grades in school, do some extracurricular activities, volunteer at a nonprofit, or get a part-time job. All of these things will make your resume look good and it is also great for college applications.

Every resume has a few things that are needed. This will help future employers know more about you and whether or not you are right for the job. You are basically selling yourself, so you need to put your best foot forward. Let's go through a few of the things that every resume should have.

Contact Details

Right at the top of your resume you will need it to have all your contact details boldly laid out. This is important because if potential employers are looking to hire you or call you in for an interview, they will need to know how to get in contact with you. Putting these at the top of your resume means that it's easy to find. Make sure these are always updated if you change your phone number or email address.

A Summary or Introduction

The next thing you should have in your resume is a summary or introduction paragraph. There only needs to be a few lines and it's basically to show potential employers what you are all about. It should show off some of your personality and why you are sending out this resume in the first place. You can tailor this section to each potential employer as this increases the chances of you getting a call back. Just changing a few details will make a huge difference.

You can use this space to showcase some skills or experience you think are especially needed in the job you are applying for.

Many potential employers or hiring managers might not read the rest of the resume if the introduction does not catch their eye. You have to remember that they will be getting tons of resumes each day, so you want to make sure yours stands out amongst the crowd.

Your Experience

Your experience section will show your potential employers what you have done in the past and that you are responsible enough to handle the job they give you. You will typically fill this with work experience, but don't worry if you don't have any. Most employers who are looking to hire teenagers, or those just graduating, will know they do not have that much experience to start with. However, you should not leave this section blank. Remember, you are trying to pitch why you are the best person for the job, so you need to fill the space with other experience that might be relevant.

It is a good time to start thinking about what you have done in the past that might have prepared you for the working world. Volunteer work is a great addition to a resume. It shows that you are responsible and that you are willing to go the extra mile. Any volunteer work is good, so if you have not done any, it is not too late to start. You can also add anything you have done for extra money. Perhaps you wash cars, walk the neighbor's dogs, or mow their lawns. Doing these kinds of activities will show that you are responsible and can work hard.

You will also need to explain what tasks you did or responsibilities you had when you had these different roles. This will help the person reading the resume get a better idea of what you did while you had these duties. Create some bullet points to make it easier to read through. You will only need three to five bullet points for each one. There is no need to over explain, especially if it was a simple task.

Any Additional Skills

You might have some special skills and talents that have not yet been showcased in the rest of the resume, so this is their time to shine. These skills will be both hard and soft skills. Hard skills are the things that you learned to do along the way. Things like working on a word document, coding, typing, or designing posters. Soft skills are the things that cannot produce something tangible like leadership skills, good communication, working well with a team, and time management.

It is important to not overdo it here. I have seen many resumes that make huge lists of their skills, and the truth is that most potential employers will not read through these large lists. It can become tiresome. The best thing to do is to tailor your skills list with the job you are applying for. You can have a separate document with all of your skills listed on it. Then when you are getting ready to send your resume out, you can look on the list for the top skills that you think they are looking for and paste these on the resume. This way you know the employer will see the most important skills for the job.

Resume Tips

If you are looking to make your resume stand out, then these tips are really going to help you out. If you follow them, then you will be able to create a great resume that people will notice. It will have all the right information and none of the extra fluff that can take away from the message.

It Only Needs to Be One Page

One of the biggest mistakes people make when they write a resume is they make it way longer than they need to. You only need it to be a page long, especially when you don't have that much work experience. In many cases, potential employees might even ignore a really long resume because they know it is going to be filled with unnecessary items. Rather, keep it simple and make sure the most important things are in there. You have a much better chance of being spotted like this. It will also cause some intrigue and make the employers want to contact you to find out more. Once you get a call or email you already have one foot in the door and all you have to do is impress them.

Keep It Simple

It can be tempting to want to make your first resume very extra but that can make things confusing. If there are too many patterns, colors, and designs it will be difficult to find the information they want. This might lead them to leave your resume to the side for a simpler one that is more straightforward.

This doesn't mean you can't add your own personality to your resume, you just have to do so sparingly. You can use color but make sure that all the colors match in some way and choose more professional ones. A resume with bright green, blue, and yellow text will probably look unprofessional and like your younger brother or sister had a hand in making it. You might feel like placing the information sporadically on the page because it looks good. While this might be true, looking good is not the main focus here. People read from top to bottom and while this is predictable it is also reliable. Someone who is reading through hundreds of resumes isn't going to want to look up and down just to find the information they want. Do your best to keep it simple and functional. This is also a lot less work for you.

Use a Template

There are tons of free templates for resumes on the internet. It makes it really easy for you to pick a design you really like and then work with it. All you have to do is fill in all of your information and edit it a bit. Then you will be good to go. There are also some better-quality templates that cost a small fee. In some cases, this is actually worth it but it is not necessary for your first resume. Just focus on getting a template that is easy to read and understand for now.

Spelling and Grammar Check

Since this is a professional document, you want to make sure you sound as professional as possible. The best thing to do is have someone else proofread it for you or to run it through a spelling and grammar software like Grammarly. This will help you pick up things you might have missed. We are all human and even if you are great at these things, there is always a chance you will miss something. You would rather have a close friend or family member find the error than a potential employer.

Tailor It to the Job Posting

The great thing about job postings of interest is that you will know what they are looking for. They will usually have a list of job responsibilities and skills that are needed in order to fulfill that role. You can have a look at these lists and see what you have that matches. Then, you can add these onto your resume so that you are able to stand out and show why you are right for the job.

One thing you should not do is lie about your skills and qualifications on your resume. This almost never turns out well. You will end up leaving a sour taste in the employer's mouth when they find out you have misrepresented yourself. Rather, be honest about the skills and experiences you have.

If You Have Good Grades, Highlight It

Any kind of academic or extracurricular achievements should be highlighted on your resume. As a teenager you won't have that much work experience to fill up the page, but you still need to show potential employers that you are responsible and capable of handling the work they need you to do. If you get straight As or are a captain of a club or group at school, make sure this is in your resume. As you get older and have more work experience you can start removing these things in order to highlight your work experience.

Check Out Examples

It is relatively easy to find examples of resumes on the internet.

All you have to do is a quick search and there will be many popping up. Take some time to search for examples of resumes for the job role that you want to apply for. This will give you a better idea of what resumes have been successful and which ones haven't. You can then do your best to replicate those resumes to give yourself a better shot.

If you cannot find example resumes on the internet, try LinkedIn. This is a professional platform where people are able to list their skills and work experience. You can connect with people who are in your desired career fields and keep up to date with their career progression. Have a look at what kind of experience, education, and skills they have that were able to land them the jobs they have. You can use this information to help build your resume.

Link Relevant Profiles

Most hiring managers will look at your social media profiles before they decide whether they are going to hire you or not. If you have public profiles, link them in your resume to save them a step. This will also show your potential employers that you have nothing to hide, and they will get to know you a bit more on a personal level. You will have to make sure that your social media accounts are professional and there isn't anything on there that might turn off a potential employer. Take some time to go through your social media profiles to make sure there isn't anything that could work against you here.

You don't have to link all your social media profiles, and you aren't required to. You can link things like your LinkedIn and Twitter, but maybe you want to keep your Instagram and TikTok private. That is fine, but just know that if you are active on social media and your profiles are public it will be pretty easy to find you. You don't want to lose a job opportunity because of something you posted.

Resume Template

Name Surname

✉ Name@myemail.com

📞 (111) 234-5678

🏠 Houston, TX

Summary:

xxx

Work Experience:

Job 1 (Date):

1. Duty 1

2. Duty 2

3. Duty 3

Job 2 (Date):

1. Duty 1

2. Duty 2

3. Duty 3

Education:

Degree Name (year completed)

- Institution

- Relevant coursework

Certificate Name (year completed)

- Institution

- Relevant coursework

High School Diploma (year completed)

- Institution

- Relevant coursework

Hard Skills:

- Skill 1

- Skill 2

- Skill 3

Soft Skills:

- Skill 1

- Skill 2

- Skill 3

You Don't Have to Have It All Figured Out

After Stacey graduated high school, she went to her dream college and studied architecture. This was something she had always been passionate about and now it was becoming a reality. She worked really hard and got good grades. Throughout her college career, her mind was focused on becoming an architect and working at one of the most prestigious architecture firms in her state.

In the summer of her final year, her uncle offered her the opportunity to work in his company until she went back to school. She decided to do it because she thought it would be a good idea to have some work experience on her resume. The company was one that provided aluminum products to big corporations. She went to work, and to her surprise, she really enjoyed it. Even more to her surprise, she was really good at it.

She enjoyed going to work in the morning and the work environment was something that really made her happy. She found that she was productive and that she was able to excel at the tasks given to her. Her manager often spoke highly of her and asked her if she would be willing to stay on after she graduated. This was not the job she had pictured herself in, but it was something she wasn't sure she wanted to give up. She knew that she would not be using her degree to its full potential, but did that really matter? Stacey was now at a crossroads. She had a big choice to make.

On the one hand she worked really hard for her degree, and on the other, she had found herself doing something she really loved. The thing about this job is that it challenged her. She was able to connect with people she never would have in the past and she was learning new skills. She could see herself climbing up the ladder and she knew it would be on her own merit. Even though it was her uncle that got her the job, he wasn't really involved in the day-to-day running of the business. With that being said, she had access to someone who could give her help and guidance on this new career path and that would potentially help her get to the top quicker.

Her manager was so pleased with her work that he was willing to offer her a really great starting salary if she came on permanently. This would be way more than she would earn as an architecture major. There was a lot to think about. Toward the end of the summer, she had a choice to make. She spent a lot of time thinking about it and asked her parents for some advice. They were pretty much happy with whatever she chose, they were supportive like that. She decided to write out a pros and cons list and eventually came to the decision that she was going to work at her uncle's aluminum company, but only for a year. Since she already knew she was good at it, she wanted to explore it a bit more. She decided that she would re-evaluate after the year was over and if she still wanted to explore architecture, then she could go into it.

Fast forward five years, she was still working at her uncle's company. She got a job offer from another big company and decided to take the job. There were no hard feelings, and she left on good terms for a better opportunity. Fast forward another ten years, and she is now working in the same industry and is incredibly happy. She was able to work her way up to a managerial position and is on track to becoming an executive. She has often thought about how different her life might have turned out if she stuck to her architecture plan, but she knows this was the right path for her.

At the end of the day, life comes with all kinds of experiences and challenges. We have to take it one day at a time. Sometimes, things will come out of the blue and you will have to make a choice. You don't have to feel as though you have to follow a specific plan. You are free to make the choices that make sense to you at the moment. Even if you don't have it all figured out right now, that's okay. Most of us don't. We make the choices that suit us best at the moment. This is not to say that you should not think things through or do your research. With Stacey, she did not make the decision to stay with the aluminum company lightheartedly. She thought about it for a long time before coming to that decision.

Staying open to opportunities that cross our paths is essential to building a future and career that we are happy with. If you have everything planned out to the exact step, you will not be able to see a good opportunity when it comes. Planning is important but so is being flexible. Planning and choosing a career can be a stressful part of a teen's life. Don't put too much pressure on yourself to have everything figured out because life has a funny way of landing you in situations you never thought you would be. Embrace it and you will see that things end up working out.

Chapter Questions and Tasks

- What experience do you have that you can add to your resume?

- Is there anything you can do to increase the amount of experience you have?

- Write out a mock resume.

PART 3

Money Management Skills

CHAPTER 11

Introduction to Money
Management

Managing your money sounds interesting, right? Okay, I know this isn't going to be the most riveting part of the journey to creating financial success, but it is one of the most important. You see, you won't have enough money to invest and grow your wealth if you don't manage your money well. Also, even if you pick the best career, you might still end up in debt and in financial stress if you can't manage the money you get from your paycheck.

The great thing about money management is that it is a skill that you will take with you throughout your life. Most adults don't even know how to manage their money because they aren't taught it. They have to make a ton of mistakes before they learn how to properly manage their money. At that point, many will be in debt and already have bad habits that need to be broken.

If you start your money management journey now, you will be able to build better habits and it will be easier when you are making a ton of money as an adult.

Important Lessons to Learn

When it comes to money management, there are many lessons to be learned. These lessons can be learned through life experience or through the stories of others. One way is far less painful than the other. Can you guess which? When we learn from the lessons of others, we are able to avoid situations that are not the best for us. The truth is that in life we are all going to make mistakes. This is pretty much a guarantee. However, we can make sure we limit those mistakes by doing what we can to avoid some of them. This is the best way to move forward in life and it will allow you to set yourself up for financial success.

In this section, we are going to go through a few of the lessons you should learn before you start managing your money. This will help you to understand why money management is important and then you will be able to make better choices in the future. For many teenagers, money and finances is not often thought about, but we are here to solve that problem.

Money Doesn't Come From Nothing

When I was a kid, my mother used to always say, "Money doesn't grow on trees!" This was usually in response to me wanting something from the toy store. As a kid, I never really thought about where money came from. It was just something that was there. The thing about money is that when we do not work hard to make it, we can take advantage of it. This is why kids will ask for the most expensive things and then get upset when their parents say no. Even when I was a teenager, I wanted stuff and used to think it was so unfair when my parents didn't buy it for me. After all, I saw all the money they had in their wallets. What's the big deal?!

When we believe that money comes from nothing or that it is easy to make it, we do not appreciate it enough. It also becomes harder for us to manage that money. If I were to give $5,000 to a child, the way they would spend it would be very different to that of an adult. A child is not aware of how money is earned, and they do not have responsibilities to think about. They have no concept of the future and would rather spend it on what they want right now. Chances are the closest toy store is going to make a large number of sales just through this one kid. An adult will understand the value of money and will likely be a lot more responsible with that money. They know how long it will take them to make the same amount and the effort it would take.

As a teenager, you probably don't have that much reference for where money comes from or what it takes to earn it. That's completely normal, but it is important to learn. As you get older, you will be able to see how much value money has. This is because you have to work for it, and you will have responsibilities that you need to pay for. If your parents give you responsibilities at home in order to earn money, then you will have a better understanding of this. If not, you can ask your parents to share their budgets and where their money is going. This will help you to fully understand personal finances and money management in a practical way. You'll be able to see how much money goes to simple things like food and electricity and why your parents might be a bit more conservative about how they spend it. It might also give you a new appreciation for them and how they choose to use their money.

Spending Happens Quicker Than Earning

Isn't it so creepy when you and your friends are talking about a brand-new piece of technology or pair of sneakers that have just come out and the next day, when you go onto social media, you get an ad for the exact same thing you were speaking about? Advertisements are now tailored to each individual person and what they search for or what they want. This means that spending money has become a whole lot easier because we are constantly being bombarded with the items that we want to buy.

Earning money typically takes a lot of time and effort from our side. We have to put in the physical and mental work in order to get paid for a specific job. This is regardless of whether we are getting $10 for a simple job or $5,000 a month. On the other hand, spending money can happen in the blink of an eye. It is much easier to spend $1,000 than to earn $1,000. When you think of it like this, you start to be a bit more conservative with your spending decisions. There are many things that we want but do not need. I'm sure you have bought tons of things that you no longer use. These things are not really valuable, and the money would have probably been a lot better off being saved or invested. The truth is, most of us will end up spending a lot of money on things that we simply do not need and that will go to waste later on. Understanding that we all have a predisposition to spending money will actually help us to protect ourselves from doing this.

There Is No Instant Gratification

When it comes to finances and money management, instant gratification is almost non-existent. Instant gratification is when you get a sense of fulfillment or pleasure out of something almost immediately. In today's world, we seek out this type of instant gratification. If we do something, then we want to be thanked or noticed for it immediately. This is actually not realistic because instant gratification is not a measure of how worthwhile something is. With this being said, there are a lot of things in our culture today that teach us to look for this instant gratification. For example, when we post something on social media, we will start getting likes and comments almost immediately and this gives a hit of dopamine to the brain that tells us what we did was good. Dopamine is the chemical in our brains that makes us feel happy and good. Another example is when we purchase something that we want. We get immediate gratification because when we get the item, the feeling of excitement overwhelms us. This makes us want to post more on social media and spend more money.

Things that actually have a long-term benefit for us do not actually give us any kind of instant gratification. Saving and investing your money isn't going to give you any kind of instant gratification because you have to leave it in your investment or savings account for a long time before you can use it. It might also take a while before you start seeing the benefits of saving and investing your money. In this case, it might feel easier to spend it on something that you want right now rather than saving it for later just because it feels good.

It is important to understand that chasing the feeling of instant gratification can get us into huge financial problems. It is far better to plan for your future rather than trying to meet all your wants in the present. This is a difficult lesson to learn and even though I am giving you this advice, it is something I also struggle with. Most of us will struggle with this but knowing that it does happen will help you to plan better in the future and hopefully you'll be able to put some habits in place that will allow you to see financial success. That is what I had to do in order to stop myself from spending money unnecessarily. I have a plan for where my money goes, and this has been incredibly helpful. This doesn't mean I don't spend it on things that I want. I just have a specific amount of money that I will use to spend on miscellaneous items, and I don't go over it. This gives me some freedom but in a controlled manner.

Borrowing and Lending Can Be Risky

We all have that one friend who is always borrowing stuff from us. It can get really annoying, but most people don't really say anything about it. While it might be okay to borrow and lend money and things for a short time, eventually it gets too much. As we get older, the money we make becomes more important to us and so does the stuff we buy; lending becomes trickier. When it comes to borrowing, there are a lot of strings attached and that makes the process harder.

Borrowing and lending of money should be avoided as much as possible as a general rule. This is because it can affect more than your financial standing. It can also impact your relationships, which is never a good thing. If you are the person who lends money to others, even if you don't have expectations on when you want the person to pay you back, there is always an underlying feeling that the other person owes you. This is a completely valid feeling but the problem with it is it can impact your relationship with the other person. Many times, people feel forced to lend money to others because they are in need. This could be due to putting yourself in a bad financial position just because you are trying to take care of someone else. It is really important that you understand the implications that come with lending money. As a teenager you are probably only lending a few dollars to your friends, and it is not going to make that much of a difference but as you get older the amount people want to borrow is going to be a lot bigger. Learning how to say no now will help you in the future because you won't feel guilty when you say no then.

When it comes to lending out money to other people, a good rule to follow is that you never do it unless you can live without that money. You should always borrow money from the excess that you have rather than making sacrifices and cutting into your budget or financial plan in order to lend money to somebody else. This will help you to not lend too much and overstretch your own budget. This is why having a budget is actually very important. You will know how much money you have left over and as soon as somebody asks to borrow money you will know whether or not you can do that.

On the emotional side of lending money out, you need to know the type of person you are. For me, I understand that when I lend money to other people I often get upset or irritated when I see them spending it on something I do not think is important. For example, when I was in college I had a friend, Jonathan, who needed some money in order to buy lunch for the week. His parents had not yet been able to deposit the money, so I decided to help him out and I lent him the amount he needed. He promised to pay me back as soon as his parents had deposited the money and everything was good. However, during that week he went out to a club, and he took his girlfriend out on a date. At any other time, he could have done these things and I wouldn't have even noticed but because I had lent him money it seemed very irresponsible for him to go out drinking at a club and taking his girlfriend out on a fancy date when he just borrowed money from me. I felt myself getting very annoyed and angry with him because of how he was spending the money.

Not only that, but it took him a little longer than what he promised to pay me back. The longer he took to give me my money back, the more irritated I was getting. Even though this might seem like a small thing, the friendship did end up suffering for it. Once I received all of my money, I decided that I was never going to lend money to him again because of the negative feelings I was having toward him. Of course, I didn't fully learn my lesson because a similar thing happened about two or three more times before I decided that lending money was simply not for me. It puts too much stress on the relationships I have with other people, and it just simply is not worth it. I find that my mind is consumed with thoughts of where my money is being spent and whether or not that person is using it for what they said they were.

You might be thinking that my thoughts were pretty justified, but the truth is that when you are in that situation you are almost consumed with thoughts of your money. It is not a very healthy place to be in, so if you are somebody that is similar to me, then perhaps lending money is something you shouldn't do. Now, there will be times when the people you love need money for something really important. I'm not saying that you should never help them out. Just recently, I had to help my sister pay for something that she simply did not have the finances to do. However, I have decided that if somebody needs money from me and I'm willing to give it to them, then I'm not going to expect it back. Rather than lending out the money, I have decided to just give it to them and save myself all the hassle. I have spoken to so many other people who have given me the same feedback in terms of this kind of situation. Sometimes giving away the money and letting it go is so much better. It will also help you to think through your decisions a lot more clearly because you do not expect to have that money back. If you are not willing to see that money go, then you should not be helping out that person in a financial way. This is a very hard lesson to learn but it really does save you a lot of heartache and stress down the line.

Okay, now that we've got the lending portion of this lesson out of the way, let's talk about borrowing. When it comes to money management, the ultimate goal is to ensure that you have enough money to sustain your current lifestyle. This means that you should not need to borrow money from anyone. Even if there was an emergency, ideally you would have enough money in your bank account to handle the emergency on your own. The scenario we spoke about above flips around when you are the person who is borrowing money. You end up indebted to the other person and until you are able to pay them back, there is always going to be some strain on the relationship. Not only that, but you just don't have freedom to spend your money the way you want to because you are always thinking about what the other person might be seeing from their point of view.

Most people who need to borrow money don't typically go to their friends and family as their first point of call. Credit and taking out loans tend to be the number-one way people borrow money. This is when the bank or financial institution gives you an advance on money so you can spend it now and then pay it back later. The issue with this is they don't give you this money for free. You need to pay back the money you owe with interest. If you're not careful, you end up being in a far worse financial position than you were to begin with. If you are in a position where you feel like you cannot afford something, look at your budget and see where you can cut back so you can free up some money. You might also decide to not purchase that item because it is not a necessity. Basically, anything that you can do to avoid taking out a loan or borrowing money is going to be much better for your financial success. In all cases, borrowing and lending money should be something you think through fully before you commit to doing it.

Your Salary Is Not That Simple

When you get a full-time job, you are going to get paid either every week, every other week, or sometimes even once a month. In the interview and when you're working through the paperwork, you will get a notice of how much your entire package is going to pay out to you. When adults say they earn X amount of money, they are talking about their entire package. However, your salary is not going to be that simple. That total amount is often not deposited into your bank account for you to distribute and spend how you please. There are multiple deductions that are taken out, so the amount that is deposited into your bank is much smaller. When you get your first job, this can be quite shocking, so it is better to prepare yourself mentally from now on.

One of the biggest expenses that you are probably going to have is paying taxes. Unfortunately, this is something that all of us have to do in order to live in the society that we live in. There is a percentage that is taken out of your salary before it even comes into your bank account. The more money you earn, the more taxes you will be paying based on that amount. This is money that you will never see because it goes straight to the government. On top of that, there might be other deductions that need to come out of your account. Some companies will have an unemployment fund that will be contributed to from your salary. Medical insurance, your retirement fund, and a few other things might also be deducted. If you get certain employee benefits, these could also be deducted from your overall salary. As you can see, the amount you might have thought you were getting is probably not the amount that you are actually getting.

When you are working out your budget, you will do so based on the money that has been deposited into your bank account and not the total amount. This way, you know exactly what you can and cannot spend. It is also important to fully understand what amount of money you will be coming home with, so when you are in an interview or in the negotiations stages of a job make sure that you are discussing these aspects. I have seen many college graduates or students who are getting their first job, and end up getting way less than they expected because of all these technicalities and deductions. You might also want to speak to your parents or guardians about what their paychecks look like and what deductions they have. This might help you get a better understanding of how money is distributed and what you can expect when you get a full-time job.

CHAPTER 12

Creating a Budget

The budget is the cornerstone of all financial planning and money management. You can't do anything without a proper budget in place. Okay, I'm lying. You might be able to make some good decisions without a budget, but it is going to be a lot harder and not as consistent. Managing your money properly is all about knowing what you have to work with and allocating it in the right places. This might sound simple, but you would be surprised at how many adults still don't get this right. Starting as soon as possible is going to be a huge benefit to you. Budgeting a few hundred dollars a month is way easier than starting off with budgeting when you are earning much more.

Create Your Budget

Creating a budget is essential for investing and life. There are so many financial problems that can be avoided when you have a budget. It allows you to be in full control of your money, so if you start when you are young and not earning a whole lot, it will be so much easier to do when you are older and earning big bucks.

You can set a budget for the week or for the month. It just depends on how your income works. The below template will be very helpful, but you can create your own. The important thing is that you start budgeting before moving onto anything else. Below is a basic template for a budget that you can use to help you get started. As you can see, there are categories for your income and expenses. Since every person's budget will look different, you will need to take some time to figure out how to fill in the necessary fields. This is the starting point for your budget, and we will be talking about the different ways you can do it in the next section.

	Expected income	Actual income
Monthly allowance		
Earnings 1		

Earnings 2		
Gifts		
Total		

Income:

Expenses:

	Planned expenses	Actual expenses	Leftover
Investments			

Savings			
Total			

The Different Budgeting Methods

As mentioned above, there are many ways you can budget your money. This is actually a good thing because we aren't all the same. Some people find certain ways of budgeting ineffective for them, so it is good to have options. You might have to try various different ways of budgeting before you find the one that works best for you. Since you are still a teen, you will be able to take your time and do this. You can figure out what works for you and what doesn't. As you get older, your budgeting preferences might change, but you will have the habit in place and that is the most important thing.

50/30/20

This is a very simple budgeting method, but it is really effective. Many people who are just starting out with budgeting use this method because it is simple to follow and there is a clear structure. The basic principle is that 50% of your money will go toward the things you need, so you are free to allocate that to the things you need to pay for each month. The 30% will go to the things that you want. You can put it toward saving for something bigger or you could spend it on the things you want to have each month. This is where the money will come from when you want an ice cream cone on a hot day or want to go out with your friends for the day. The final 20% is going toward your savings or paying off debt. At this point in your life, you are unlikely to have any debt, so it will be purely savings and investments.

This split will allow you to save for the future but also have enough to spend on your wants and needs in the present. You will still get a chance to enjoy the money you earn. I have seen many people try to save a majority of their money by cutting so much of the stuff they want. They are able to do it for a short while but often have to give it up because they cannot enjoy their money. It can get pretty miserable to keep saying no to friends or never being able to buy something just because you want it. Doing these kinds of things makes life interesting and fun and you shouldn't be so strict with yourself that you never get to enjoy these aspects of life. It really is all about balance.

The 50/30/20 is split up this way because it is realistic for most people, but you should not feel pressured to stick to these percentages. You might not have a lot of expenses because you know your parents take care of everything you need. This means you have more money to put toward your wants and your savings or investments. Work it out in a realistic way so that you are able to enjoy a part of your money but save and invest as much as you can. As you move through life, you can continue changing the percentages to suit your needs.

Cash Envelope System

Some people find it really difficult to budget when their money is in their bank account. This requires you to keep track of all your spending and it can get very tedious. You might also get most of your income from cash-based sources and perhaps you don't want to deposit it into the bank unless you have to. Investments and savings will be better off in the bank, but the rest of your cash you can put in envelopes and use this method of budgeting.

For the cash envelope system, you will need envelopes (go figure!). Each envelope will have a specific category in your budget. For example, you could have separate envelopes for school supplies, food, going out with friends, and clothes. You will put a specific amount of cash in each of them. You will only use the cash in each envelope for that specific task. Once the money in the envelope is finished, you will no longer be able to spend it in that category. If you get close to the end of the month and you realize you are under budget, you can move the leftover money to where you need it at the moment. This makes budgeting very tangible, and you are working with a specific amount for each category.

This is a great method for when you are first starting out with budgeting because of the fact that you are working with real money. It can be difficult to work with money if you can't physically see it. We always think we have more than we actually do, and this can get us in trouble. Doing it this way will allow you to be more thoughtful when you are spending your money. You also won't risk overspending because you can only spend the cash you have with you. If you struggle with overspending when you are out and about, then this is another reason to use this method.

Zero-Based Budgeting

If you are looking to have full control of your money, then this is the budgeting method for you. You are basically budgeting right down to zero. This means that you will not have any money left over. This does not mean that you can't have some money for a spontaneous milkshake every now and then, these types of things are just all planned into the budget. You might put aside a certain amount of money for spontaneous events, and once you have reached that limit you cannot spend anymore. This allows you to have full control over everything that goes on with your money.

If you are using a bank card to make all your transactions, then you will have to log each and every time you spend your money. The best way to do this is with an app or using a spreadsheet. There are tons of apps out there that connect with your bank account and categorize your spending. These can be very helpful, so you don't have to do this manually. Some people are not comfortable with using an app, so a spreadsheet is the best way to go. You can connect to the sheet on your phone and make additions as you spend. Keeping track of spending is the only way this method is going to work.

If you struggle with this, you can use cash to aid you in your spending. This will allow you to have more control and you don't have to log everything. This might be easier when you first get started. The zero-based budget is great when you have a specific goal because you can put more money into the things that are important to you.

Budgeting Tips and Tricks

Budgeting can be difficult when you first do it. This is why having a few tips and tricks can be very helpful. You can use the ones that work best for you or use them all. Since budgeting is such an individual thing, you will have to figure out how to make it work best for you.

Set a Date Each Month

Budgeting should be made a priority in everybody's life, but sometimes life can get busy and you forget. This is why setting a date on your calendar to fit with your budget is going to be so helpful. Doing this on the same day and time each month is going to help you build a habit. When it is a habit, it will be easier for you to continue on with. You can also set a reminder for this, so you don't forget.

Budgeting will get easier and the time you spend will be shorter as you continue doing it. Most months are very similar, so the bulk of your budget will already be taken care of. Then you only have to worry about where to allocate money for the smaller things. This process might only take you a few minutes, so you don't have to worry about sitting around for hours crunching the numbers.

Most Important to Least

The order in which you start budgeting is very important because you might realize that you do not have the amount of money you thought you did. You will need to make sure the most important things are covered first so that you know where you can make some sacrifices. For example, you know that your savings and investments are going to be the most important things for you. The money for this will need to be allocated first. Then you can start budgeting for the things you know you will need for the month. Once this is done, you can look into budgeting for the things that are not necessities. Things like going to the movies or buying a new video game. These things might be fun, and you would want them, but they are not high up on the priority list. You can then see how much money you have to spare and perhaps save up so that you can buy that video game the next month.

Keep Making Changes

Once you have your budget laid out, you can see how it goes for the first month or so. After that you might need to see where you can make some changes. There might be areas you can cut back on so that you can reach your goals faster. If you really want to save up some money so that you can go on vacation with your friend, you will need to make sure you can allocate money to this savings goal. You should set a number for you to reach in the next few months, then look at your budget and see how you can accommodate your new goal.

The first place that budget cuts will need to happen is with all the fun stuff that is not a necessity. This doesn't mean that you can never do anything fun, but you might need to be a bit more creative with how you handle your money and spend time with your friends. For example, if you and your friends are planning on going out to the movies and you know this is going to be expensive, why not invite everyone over to your house to watch a movie there? You could ask your parents if you could have the TV room for the night and make it a fun night with snacks and maybe even have a sleepover. Honestly, this sounds like a great idea because you can stay home and not have to put in the energy to get dressed and ready to go outside, but maybe this is showing my age! Staying in is definitely the more attractive option in my head! Moving on… Staying at home will allow you to have the same fun night with your friends and it isn't going to cost you any money. Let's be honest, all the snacks that you are going to be serving your friends are coming out of your kitchen, which means they are already paid for. You can also ask everyone to bring something. There are lots of ways to cut down on your budget and still be able to enjoy yourself. You just need to be a little creative.

Always Have a Buffer Amount

Even if you are using the zero-based budgeting method, having a buffer amount is going to help you out a lot. A buffer amount is a small amount that you set aside just in case. You will quickly realize that it is almost impossible to stick to your budget 100%. Things might happen that are completely out of your control. Perhaps the price of gas increases overnight and now the amount you budgeted for is too little. Maybe your little brother is upset about something that happened at school and you want to take him out for ice cream to cheer him up. There are so many things that could just happen, including not budgeting the right amount because you did not have all the correct information.

Having a certain amount that is just there in case you need a little extra will prevent you from stealing from other areas of your budget. If you have to take from another area, you might need to sit down and redo the whole budget, and this can be time consuming and unmotivating. If it comes to the end of the month and you do not need your buffer amount, then you can put it into your savings or treat yourself with it.

Try Out a Budgeting App

Budgeting apps really make things a lot easier for you especially if you are using a bank account for the majority of your spending. These apps have been designed to work with your bank account in order to categorize all of your spending and show you exactly where your money is going. Typically, connecting to your bank account is an optional thing, so if you are not comfortable with that, you can choose to manually enter all of your information into the budgeting app. This is going to take a little more time from your day, but at least you'll have peace of mind, and you can make logging a habit.

There are tons of budgeting apps but each of them will have different benefits and drawbacks so make sure that you do research so you can pick the right one for you. Another thing to consider is whether or not you are willing to pay a premium for the budgeting apps. There are a few really good ones that do require a paid subscription service, but this might not be necessary, and it could be way too expensive for your current budgeting needs. There are also some really great free ones, so make sure you have checked all of them out and used the trial period, so you can fully understand how they work and whether it's going to be a good option for you.

Chapter Questions and Tasks

- Which budgeting method do you think would work best for you?

- Make a list and prioritize what you spend your money on.

- Do some research on budgeting apps and find one that is going to suit your needs the best.

Chapter 13

Saving and Spending Wisely

Being able to manage your money properly means that you have to prioritize saving and ensure that you are spending on the right things. If you are used to simply spending your money on whatever you want at the moment, then this might be a big change for you. It is actually going to be a change for the better because it teaches you self-control and you will definitely need this skill as you get older. It will help you in many different areas of your life and you can show that you are a responsible person and know where your priorities lie. You also won't fall victim to any marketing schemes or advertising that you see around.

Create an Emergency Fund

An emergency fund is one of the best things you can create for yourself. This is something that will allow you to have peace of mind with your finances. Even though you probably don't have a lot to be financially worried about right now, creating this emergency fund will help you out in the future. Life is very unexpected and sometimes you will need to fork out some cash on a large, unexpected emergency. This is where the fund comes in handy. For adults, these emergencies will be things like a burst water pipe in the home, their dog needs to be rushed to the vet, or there is an unexpected expense needed for their child. You might not have all of these things, but creating an emergency fund is a habit that you can build, not that will benefit you later.

Perhaps you don't have to call it an emergency fund. You might want to call it a just-in-case fund. This can cover a whole lot of scenarios where you need money just in case. For example, your favorite artist announces their new tour dates, and you really want to buy a ticket to the show. You can take some money out of your just-in-case fund and purchase the tickets early. Then you can put the money back into the fund over the course of the next few months. The goal is to have enough money in your fund to carry you through any kind of situation that might not be foreseen. Once you have that money in the fund you don't have to worry about putting anything extra in until you spend it. Then you'll have to work on putting the money back into the fund and the cycle will repeat itself. It's basically like money that you will loan yourself at different periods in your life.

When you get older, you will already have the habit of saving into a type of emergency fund and it will be a lot easier to continue with this practice. When you make your first full salary, you should aim to have at least three-to-six-months' worth of your expenses in your emergency fund. This will also help protect you financially should you lose your job or source of income. You would have three to six months to find something else, so you don't have to stress out and choose a job just because it's the first one available. This gives you a bit more freedom to make the choices that you are happy with and not be forced into anything just because you don't have enough money.

Cut Down on Eating Out

Did you know that a majority of Americans eat out multiple times a week? This might be you and your family, and the truth is that this is probably eating away at a lot of your money. If your parents can afford it, then that's perfectly okay but you should look at how much money you spend on eating out every month. You probably don't need to spend any money on food as your parents take care of the bulk of it. There is also nothing wrong with you going out a few times with your friends to have something to eat. However, it does become a problem when you are spending the majority of your money on eating out when you can save that money and put it toward something else.

Most fast-food restaurants will sell food that is well under $10; that makes it very easy to justify quickly going to a McDonald's or Burger King in order to grab something. If you do this multiple times a month, or multiple times a week, then this can really add up to a large sum of money. Not to mention that this is probably not the healthiest for your body. Try working this habit out of your life so that you do not have to worry about burning excess on eating out unnecessarily.

One of the goals that really helped me to kick this habit was to only eat out when I was in a social setting. Only if I had my friends with me would I go to a restaurant or to a fast-food joint. This meant that it became an event that I truly enjoyed taking part in because I'm spending time with people that I like. I was able to save a whole lot of money toward the other goals that were more important to me. Try this out and see if it works for you as well.

Do You Really Need More Clothes?

Most of us want to make a good impression and look good. There is truly nothing wrong with that, but it does come at a cost. You probably don't need to buy clothes every single month as you will likely have everything you need. Most of the time when we are buying clothes, it's not because we actually need them, but because we want to keep up with the trends and just purchase something new. You can buy new clothes every now and then, but it doesn't have to be something that you spend your money on each month. Doing this can actually put a drain on your bank account and it is quite unnecessary.

One of my good friends put boundaries in place around this because she really enjoyed purchasing new clothes. She realized that a lot of her clothes were actually going to waste because she didn't have places to wear them to or she had something very similar in her wardrobe already. What she did to combat spending excess money on her clothing, was to put together a plan. She looked inside her closet to see what she was wearing and what she needed. For an entire month, she turned all of her hangers facing in one direction and every time she wore an item of clothing, she would put it back on the hanger in the other direction. This helped her to visually see what she was wearing and what didn't fit her style anymore. She gave it a few more months for a few of the items but most of them she donated or threw out. Then she was left with a closet full of items that she actually does wear and enjoys wearing.

From here, she started writing out a list of the clothing items that she needed in order to make her closet better. She wasn't allowed to purchase any clothing items unless it was on that list. If it was on the list, she knew that she thought about it before going to the store or ordering it online. Now she doesn't go to the store and feel like she needs to impulse buy items because if it's not on the list, she simply ignores it. She has ended up saving a lot of money on her clothing and I think this is great practice for anyone who is struggling to do the same.

Avoid Impulse Spending

Impulse spending can secretly get you and the problem with it is that you don't notice that it's happening. An impulse is when you suddenly feel the need to do something or buy something. This is typically driven by emotions. Let's look at the clothing example one more time. If you go to your favorite clothing store and you didn't intend to buy anything, but you saw a T-shirt or pair of jeans that look amazing, you might be very tempted to purchase that item. This is not an item that you need, but it's something that you really want at the moment because it has made you excited.

These items are hardly ever things that are important to you, and they will most likely just sit in your room collecting dust. To help prevent yourself from impulsive spending, you will need to put some sort of plan in place. What you can do is decide that whenever you feel like buying something you are going to give it a few days to think about it. If you still want that item after a few days, you can go back and get it. If the excitement has died down, then you know that this was an impulse decision and you do not need the item. You will probably not even think about it after you leave the store or exit the website. Now you have saved a nice chunk of money to use for something else that really is important to you.

It's Not Worth It to Try Impress Others

Throughout life you are probably going to be tempted to show off or want to purchase things just because other people have them. You might think this is just a problem that people your age have, but even adults go through this. Nobody is exempt from trying to impress others with what they have or what they can afford. However, this hardly ever turns out well because when you try to live above your means in order to have people be impressed by you, you end up being very unhappy. Sometimes we do this without even realizing it and that is why it's important to catch yourself in the act and cut off the habit.

There will always be somebody who has more than you or who expects more from you and if you keep trying to live up to those kinds of expectations then you're always going to be financially unsuccessful. The only way you can become financially successful is if you are able to manage your money properly. Managing your money is all about taking what you have and making it work for your current lifestyle. This might mean that you have to make some sacrifices at certain points in your life in order not to overspend. You might even need to make some cutbacks in your current lifestyle in order to fit into what your finances can allow. As a teenager, your financial situation is probably not going to have that much of an impact on your lifestyle. However, it is a good lesson to learn as soon as possible so that you don't try and impress people and then end up getting yourself into debt.

It is an important lesson to learn from an early age. You don't always have to have the newest shoes or smartphone. The things that seem so important right now are probably not going to matter within the next 10 years. A good question you should ask yourself before you make large purchases or start thinking about buying something new is whether or not this thing will matter in the next year or so. If it doesn't matter in the future, then it's not important enough for you to have it right now.

You also need to take into consideration who you are trying to impress. If the majority of the people you are trying to impress will not be in your life in the next few years, then there's no point in trying to impress them in any case. Most of the people in your school will lose touch with you and you will not see them ever again after graduation. This means within the next few years, whatever you accumulated to impress your classmates won't even matter. You won't even know these people so what they think of you shouldn't even be something you think about. The people who truly care about you will be the ones you do not need to impress because you can be yourself around them. It's not about what you have but who you are. In fact, not having nice things is a great way to see who is in your life for the right reasons. The people who don't care about your status or how many fancy things you have are the people you want in your life, and these will be the people who remain friends for many years to come.

This can be a tough lesson to learn because we all want people to like us and even as adults, we want to have some level of popularity. Having other people like us is a nice feeling, but it's not the ultimate goal and it should never be. We should be focused on our own character instead and building up our own lives rather than thinking about what other people think about us. Having these thoughts consuming your minds means that we can never step into the success that is hopefully waiting for us in the future.

Social media has made it even easier for us to compare ourselves to other people and for us to try and impress others. We post things on social media just to look good and portray a certain lifestyle even though it is not a hundred percent true. Social media is the highlight reel of our lives and not the full representation of it. It is important not to look at other people's highlight reel and compare your life to it. You are looking at all the best parts that they are choosing to show the world and comparing it to your worst moments. You also don't know what they have to do to get the things they have and sometimes it's not going to be worth it. This is why it is so much better for you to stay focused on your own dreams and goals and make plans to meet them that are going to be realistic for your starting point. Your life can be anything you want it to be but comparing yourself to other people and getting caught up in all the highlights on social media is definitely not the way to do it.

Chapter Questions and Tasks

- Write down three things you can do to save more money.

- What was the last thing you purchased? Was it an impulse buy, or did you think it through?

- Go through your room and find a few items you bought that you no longer use. Think about how much they cost and whether you think it was worth it.

CHAPTER 14

Credit and Debt Management

As a teenager, you probably don't know that much about debt or credit. This is actually a good thing because it means that you are starting with a clean slate. Debt is a massive problem in today's society and many adults struggle with it for many years. It causes them a lot of stress and heartache, and it doesn't put them in the best position for financial success. The worst part is that getting into debt is so easy these days. Many people find themselves in debt before they even know what to do with it. On top of that, many people do not even understand what it is, let alone how to get out of it. In this chapter we are going to go through all things debt and credit management so that you do not fall into any of the common traps we see people in all the time.

The Infamous Student Loan Debt

One of the biggest forms of debt that has taken hold of our

society is student loan debt. This is when a student takes out a loan from a bank or other financial services provider and promises to pay it back once they have graduated and gotten a job. This sounds like a great idea because the student does not have to pay for their studies until they're earning a salary. The problem with this is the interest on student loan debt could potentially be incredibly high. There's also no guarantee that the person will get a high-paying job after they have graduated from college. This means that the average person is already in a large amount of debt and owes a huge amount of money before they even start working. If you follow in those footsteps, then you will end up being on the financial backfoot which is definitely not where you want to be.

The price of education is increasing year-over-year and that means that it is very expensive for the average student to study what they want to. On top of that, many of the high-paying jobs require some sort of degree in order to get your foot in the door. You can never predict the type of life that you will have after you graduate and taking out a huge amount of debt is going to put unnecessary pressure on you. You will not have the freedom you would like to make certain choices about your career and your life. Student loan debt is also something that can follow you around for many years. I have friends who have had student debt that they have been paying off since their early 20s. Even though they might be married with children of their own, they're still paying off this debt they took out when they were much younger. This puts unnecessary strain on their family and their finances.

I'm not trying to say that student loans are all bad. There are definitely some good aspects to taking a student loan. The biggest benefit is that you are able to study what you want to study without having to worry about finances at the moment. The major problem comes with how we handle student loan debt and how we look at it. Most people think of a student loan as a normal thing and not something you should look into if you have no other option. I believe that there are plenty of ways in which you can fund your studies without taking out student loans or at least lessening the amount of student debt you take on. We will be talking more about this in the next section.

Let's take a break before the next section and go over a debt story that happened to one of my cousins. This should help you understand why student debt is not a great idea. Tristan always wanted to study at one of the top colleges in the country. He was accepted into an ivy league school and jumped at the opportunity without a second thought. He was also accepted into another college where the cost of tuition would have been almost half, but after receiving his acceptance letter from Yale, he had the blinders on. He took out a student loan and he was ready to go. Whenever we would meet up in semester breaks, he would be wearing his Yale sweater and gushed about how amazing campus life was. He was part of the elite, and he knew it. I wish I could say that I was not jealous, but every so often the green-eyed monster would rear its ugly head.

Anyway, after he had graduated, he got a job just like the rest of us. Granted, his was slightly higher paying but after about two or three years out of college, Yale just became a story he told. It didn't really matter because we were all on the same playing field. We all had jobs and careers. In the workforce, a good degree from a great institution can be really helpful when you start but hard work actually matters more. The one major difference was that he had a lot of debt to pay off that some of us didn't because we chose a different path for education. Even with the higher salary he made, he would still be bringing home less than I would just because of the student loan repayments. He is in his 30s now and is still paying off his student loan. He probably still owes around $100,000 on the loan, so it just seems like it's never ending.

Being stuck in debt for over 10 years can seem incredibly overwhelming and it really is. The sad truth is that there are so many Americans that are in the same boat. I know of people who are in their 50s and 60s that are still paying off this debt. The reason debt is so scary is because you can never predict what is going to happen in the future. What if you get sick and have to take time off work for a year? You might really want to take a sabbatical and travel but can't because you need to pay off your student loan. Or you might be looking to start a family at some point and the amount of student debt you have could be getting in the way of that. Debt is simply taking a money issue and giving it to your future self. It restricts your choices and your freedom. If there are ways you can avoid debt, I would suggest you do that because the dark cloud that debt is capable of casting over your life is something that nobody wants.

How to Avoid Student Loan Debt

Many people believe that they do not have a choice when it comes to student debt. If they want to study and get a degree, then they will need to take out some form of debt in order to pay for it. This is actually not true. There are various options that can be looked at in order to avoid student debt completely or to lower the amount that you need to take out. This will help you and your parents plan for your studies and ensure that neither of you are putting yourself in a financial hole.

Start Saving Early

One of the best things you can do for your college tuition is to start saving as early as possible. If you are in school right now, then you have a few years before you get started with college. This means you have some time in order to save up as much money as you can. You can plan this with your parents so that you put yourself in the best position for when you start college. Ask them if they have a college fund for you and how much money is going to be available. This way you will have all the information you need to plan how much you will need to raise for your own college tuition.

You have to remember that college is not just the tuition fees that will need to be paid. You will also need to pay for books, supplies, and possibly housing as well as food. All of these things really add up and can be unexpected if you have not researched it. If you have a specific college in mind, it would be a good idea to have a look at their fees as well as their accommodation costs. This way you are able to plan better, and you can fully understand what the cost of college actually is.

Choose the Right School

There are so many options when it comes to colleges that you are actually going to be spoiled for choice. Most people want to pick the most prestigious or most expensive college, and this can actually be a mistake. While it can look good on your resume that you attended an ivy league school, it is definitely not a necessity for you to land a good job. There are many people who went to these prestigious schools and are working a regular job. The only time you can fully justify going to one of the schools is if there is a degree or course that is specialized or only offered at that school. If you are studying something a bit more general, then you can go to any college that will offer you the best deal.

It is essential that you do your research and compare prices among the different kinds of schools. I know people who have hacked the system because they decided to go to community college for the first year or two of their degree and then transfer to a more prestigious school. This means they still get their degree from the prestigious school, but they have saved a lot of money since two years were spent at community college which is definitely a lot cheaper. The quality of education at community and smaller colleges is still really good, so most of the time you are just paying for the name or the brand of the ivy league or prestigious college.

If you are planning on trying this hack, make sure that the community college you have applied to will transfer credit to the more prestigious school. It is quite easy to find that information if you contact both colleges and find out how the process works. This will help you to plan and prepare in advance.

Apply for Scholarships or Grants

There are many scholarships and grants out there that will pay for your studies or at least pay a portion of it. All you have to do is apply for them and then meet the requirements set out. Certain scholarships or grants might require you to work for a specific company for a stipulated amount of time in order to get it. This can actually be a good thing because it means that you have landed your first job before you even started studying. It will also keep you motivated to keep your grades up because you need to do this in order for the scholarship to keep paying for your studies. Do some research and find out what scholarships or grants are being offered for which degrees. This might also help you choose which degree to study.

Living at Home

I know the dream for many college students is to move far away from their parents' home and have a whole lot of new experiences, but that can actually be costly. I think it is really important for you to start thinking about why you want to go to college. Is it simply for all the new experiences or is it to get a degree that you can build a career from? If it is for the experience, you have to think about whether that is enough to justify getting into hundreds of thousands of dollars in debt.

The reason I bring this up is because I have noticed that there are a lot of teenagers who want to go to college for the party life instead of actually studying and building their career. The original point of going to college was to equip you for your adult life and help you to get the job of your dreams. Now that we seem to have entered into this culture where the experience of college is more important than the skills and knowledge you will gain from it, it really begs the question of whether or not college is actually worth it. I'm not arguing for or against going away to college or having the experiences that college brings but it is worth thinking about and working through this on your own.

The truth is that if you are after the experience that college brings, you can probably get a similar experience without having to pay that much money. A community college will allow you to have the same college experience but at a fraction of the cost. If you are after the independence factor, then perhaps getting a job or taking an internship outside of your current city would be a better choice. This way you are able to get the experience that you're after. but you do not have to get in debt to do it. You will also be adding some job experience to your resume, which is always a good thing. Once you have had the experiences that you are after you can decide whether or not going to college is going to be the best route for you.

You might even decide that distance learning is the option for you. This is when you basically study from home through an accredited college or tertiary education facility. You can still get a degree or diploma from these institutions, but you do not have to go into campus every day. This cuts down the amount of money you will need to pay for your tuition. It also gives you the flexibility to work a part-time or full-time job while you are studying. There are many people who do this, and I can argue for the fact that they end up being better prepared for the workforce because they are doing two things at the same time. By the time they graduate with a four-year degree they also have four years of work experience to add to the resume. For many job roles, this is going to be incredibly beneficial and can give you a leg up on the competition. It also shows that you are disciplined enough to study on your own without the supervision of a lecturer.

FAFSA

FAFSA stands for Free Application for Federal Student Aid. There are many financial-aid programs that are only granted to students from households who earn below a certain amount. With the FAFSA, anyone can apply. The great thing about this is that you don't even need to know which school you want to go to in order to apply for this. You should fill out an application as soon as possible as this will give you the best chance of hearing back and seeing what options are available in terms of financial aid. How much you will get will depend on the school as well as the criteria set out, but it really doesn't hurt to apply and see what happens. You should apply for this every single year as this is not the type of financial aid that gets renewed.

Paying Off Debt

Whoops! You found yourself in debt, now what? The truth is many people find themselves in debt by accident even if they have put a lot of parameters in place to avoid it. If you do end up in debt in the future, it is definitely not the end of the world. There are things that you can do and put into place that can help you pay off your debt and get yourself back into good financial standing. If you do end up in debt, getting out of it is going to be your number one financial goal. You can put the rest of your financial goals on the back burner for now until you can fully pay off your debt. This is because it works on an interest-rate basis and the longer you leave your debt hanging there, the more it will accumulate. Even if you save and invest, you are working against a negative number when you are in debt. Paying that off first and then focusing on your savings and investments will help you to get to a positive financial standing a lot quicker.

There are many different strategies that you can use in order to help get yourself out of debt. These strategies depend on the type of person you are and what you think will help you. We're going to talk about two of the most popular debt payoff strategies and why they work so well. It is important to note that they are both effective, so you will have to look at your own situation and your own personality to decide which one is going to be the most beneficial for you.

Debt Avalanche

The first strategy is called the debt avalanche strategy. While it might have a funny name, this can be incredibly effective in helping you pay off your debt and reducing the interest you pay in the long-term. What you want to do is make a list of all the debt that you have accumulated throughout the years. You might have various forms of debt including credit cards, student loan, store credit, etc. Make a list of all of your debt and then put it in order of the highest to lowest interest rate.

Once you have your list written out, you will start by paying the minimum amount on all of your debt. Once this is done, you will then free up any extra money and pay it toward the debt with the highest interest rate. Once that is completely paid off, you will move on to the second one that's on the list. You will put the majority of the money into the second one on the list until it is fully paid off and then we'll move on until you have completely paid off all your debt on the list.

This method is great because it saves you a ton of money. The first type of debt you will be working on will be the one that is draining the most money away from you. Since you are not leaving it to accumulate interest over the long-term, you are going to be saving quite a bit. This method is great for anyone who has a lot of extra money to give toward paying off their debt and is disciplined enough to stick to it. Debt can take a long time to completely get rid of and typically the one with the highest interest rate might be the one that takes the longest to pay off. This means that it might not seem like you're making that much of a dent in your debt for quite a long time. The psychological aspect of this is it can be very unmotivating. Making sure you are mentally prepared to be disciplined until all your debt is paid off is essential for this method.

Debt Snowball

The next debt payoff method is called the debt snowball. I know, all of these names make you want to start skiing on the Alpine Slopes. Besides the funny names, these methods are very effective. OK, so the debt snowball method is slightly different from the previous one we have discussed. With this method you will still need to list out all the debt that you have to pay back, but the order is going to be slightly different. Your list will be from the smallest amount of debt to the largest amount of debt that you need to pay off. You do not have to concern yourself with the interest rate you will be paying back on each of the debt because that is not going to be a huge factor here.

Once you have your list, you will also start paying off all the debt with the minimum amount needed. Once you have done that, you will take any extra money you have and pay it into the smallest amount of debt that you have. Since this is the smallest amount, you should be able to be paid off the quickest. Once that is paid off you will take all the money you have been paying in the smallest amount of debt and put it toward the second smallest. As you move down the list, the amount of money you are freeing up to pay off each debt is going to get larger and larger. This is why it's called the snowball method. Eventually, you will start to pay off your debt a lot quicker because you have this large amount of money to work with. It is also incredibly motivating, because you get to tick off all the debt that you are paying off and see it being removed from the list. This has a psychological effect on a person and makes it more likely that they will stick to this method. There is some sort of gratification that comes from crossing off the debt on your list.

If you are somebody who has struggled to pay off debt in the past, or you know that you need this kind of psychological motivation, then this is the debt payoff method for you. Even though it doesn't have the interest benefits the avalanche method does, it definitely helps you to stay on track. The most important thing is that you have a plan to pay off your debt. It doesn't really matter which method you choose; you just have to choose the one that is going to work best for you and the one that you can actually stick to.

You can use the following chart to help keep track of your debt and how much you need to pay.

Type of debt	Amount owed	Min. payment	Ideal payment	New balance					
				Month 1	Month 2	Month 3	Month 4	Month 5	Month 6

Credit Cards

Building your credit score is actually really important because it allows you to have more leverage with your finances. Now we have already spoken about how debt can be a bad thing, but you might need credit or debt in order to make larger purchases that could be financially beneficial. For example, if you want to buy a property later on in your life the chances of you having all the money you need to make the purchase is very small. This is because property is incredibly expensive. In this case, it is a good idea to take out a home loan and then pay it back as soon as possible. Since real estate is an investment for the future, this can be thought of as a form of good debt. It can be difficult to get a home loan if you do not have a good credit score. Working on your credit score from a young age definitely has its benefits.

One of the best ways to create a healthy credit score is to have a credit card. The trick is to use it properly so that you don't get yourself into debt that you can't get yourself out of. A credit card should be used as a tool to build your credit score and not as a form of free money. Many people get themselves into a bad situation because they use a credit card and are unable to pay it back. If you pay back whatever you spend on your credit card each month, then you are able to build your credit score without getting into debt. The thing with a credit card is when you spend the money on it the financial institution will charge you interest if you do not pay back in time. This means you could end up paying a lot more money when using a credit card. However, if you pay it back at the end of the month or before the next credit cycle, then you will not be met with any interest to pay back.

There are tons of credit cards that are available to teenagers. You will just need your parents to help you open it, but after that you can learn how to manage your own credit. Chase, Capital One, and American Express all have credit cards that are available to teenagers. These are just some of the examples of financial institutions that do carry these types of credit cards, but it is important to do your own research so you can weigh out the pros and cons of each. If you are unable to get your own credit card, you can also ask your parents to add you as an authorized user on theirs so that you are able to utilize their credit card. They will be able to see all the transactions and also have full control over the card, so if you do go overboard, then they will be able to help you out and it will be a lesson learned.

If you are a visual learner, then perhaps it would be beneficial for you to ask your parents to get involved in teaching you more about credit and taking out loans. Ask your parents to loan you a certain amount of money and charge you interest if you are unable to pay back by a certain amount of time. Purposely don't pay back the money in time and see how the interest increases the amount you owe to your parents. You will realize how quickly this can all add up and result in you paying a huge amount of money even if you took out a small amount. The thing with credit and debt is that it often spirals out of control without the person even noticing it. Visually understanding how this happens can allow you to better plan and avoid this in your own life.

Chapter Questions and Tasks

- What is debt?

- List out three ways you plan on lowering the amount of student loan debt you need to take on.

- What credit cards are available to teenagers in your area? List out a few pros and cons for each.

Conclusion

It is never too early to start working on your financial success. It can be easy to leave all the financial stuff to the adults, but almost every adult would tell you that they wished they had started earlier. Whether it is with investing or just planning for your future, you can start now. Taking the first step was picking up this book and from here on out, you will have to start taking action with what you have learned.

There might have been a particular chapter that stood out for you. Perhaps this is where you need to start. Take some time to decide where you want to start implementing steps for your financial success. Every person is different, so their plan going forward will be different. However, the most important thing is that you get moving on this journey. Financial success is within your grasp, no matter your age. Your teen years are just perfect for you to set up your foundation.

Thank You

Before you leave, I'd just like to say, thank you so much for purchasing my book.

I spent many days and nights working on this book so I could finally put this in your hands.

So, before you leave, I'd like to ask you a small favor.

Would you please consider posting a review on the platform? Your reviews are one of the best ways to support indie authors like me, and every review counts.

Your feedback will allow me to continue writing books just like this one, so let me know if you enjoyed it and why. I read every review and I would love to hear from you. Simply visit the link below to leave a review.

References

Adams, D. (2020, November 27). *How to teach your teens about credit*. Forbes Advisor. https://www.forbes.com/advisor/credit-score/teaching-teens-about-credit/

Adams, R. (2023, January 3). *Start investing as A teenager + what you should invest in*. Young and the Invested. https://youngandtheinvested.com/best-investments-for-teenagers/

Baluch, A. (2022, March 23). *Everything you need to know about allowances for kids*. The Balance. https://www.thebalancemoney.com/what-is-the-average-allowance-for-kids-4177812

Barnett, A. (2023, June 31). *Best credit cards for teens of 2023: 6 cards for beginners*. Money under 30. https://www.moneyunder30.com/best-credit-cards-for-teens

Better Money Habits. (n.d.). *Creating a budget with a personal budget spreadsheet*. Better Money Habits. https://bettermoneyhabits.bankofamerica.com/en/saving-budgeting/creating-a-budget

Better Money Habits. (2022). *Saving money tips - 8 simple ways to save money*. Better Money Habits. https://bettermoneyhabits.bankofamerica.com/en/saving-budgeting/ways-to-save-money

Buj, M. (n.d.). *11 tips for career planning at any age or career stage.* LiveCareer. https://www.livecareer.com/resources/careers/planning/career-planning-tips

Corporate Finance Institute. (2023, January 23). *Money management.* Corporate Finance Institute. https://corporatefinanceinstitute.com/resources/capital-markets/money-management/

Cruze, R. (2022, July 14). *15 practical budgeting tips.* Ramsey Solutions. https://www.ramseysolutions.com/budgeting/the-truth-about-budgeting

Dautaj, J. (2018, December 12). *Career planning for teens.* LoveToKnow. https://teens.lovetoknow.com/Career_Planning_for_Teens

DiLallo, M. (2023, January 9). *Investment guide for teens and parents with teens.* The Motley Fool. https://www.fool.com/investing/how-to-invest/investing-for-teens/

Doyle, A. (2022, March 31). *Sample resume for a part-time teen position with writing tips.* The Balance. https://www.thebalancemoney.com/part-time-job-resume-example-for-a-teen-2063248

Easy Peasy Finance. (2020, October 30). *What is investing? A simple explanation for kids, teens & beginners.* Easy Peasy Finance. https://www.easypeasyfinance.com/investing-for-kids-financial-literacy/

Eneriz, A. (2022, April 13). *Debt avalanche vs. debt snowball: What's the difference?* Investopedia. https://www.investopedia.com/articles/personal-finance/080716/debt-avalanche-vs-debt-snowball-which-best-you.asp

Freeman, A. (2016, September 27). *16 ways to reduce & avoid overwhelming college student loan debt.* Moneycrashers.com. https://www.moneycrashers.com/reduce-avoid-student-loan-debt/

Geier, B. (2021, February 10). *10 types of investments (and how they work)*. SmartAsset. https://smartasset.com/investing/types-of-investment

Gobler, E. (2022, June 20). *Investing guide for teens (and parents)*. The Balance. https://www.thebalancemoney.com/investing-guide-for-teens-and-parents-4588018

Gorton, D. (2021, October 14). *Taxes definition*. Investopedia. https://www.investopedia.com/terms/t/taxes.asp

Herrity, J. (2023, January 5). *Choosing a career path in 9 steps*. Indeed. https://www.indeed.com/career-advice/finding-a-job/choosing-a-career-path

Huang, E. (n.d.). *10 money management tips for teens*. Echo Wealth Management. https://www.echowealthmanagement.com/blog/10-money-management-tips-teens

Indeed. (2022a, June 4). *14 effective career planning tips for professionals*. Indeed. https://ca.indeed.com/career-advice/career-development/career-planning-tips

Indeed. (2022b, June 30). *Resume examples for teens: Template and writing tips*. Indeed. https://www.indeed.com/career-advice/resumes-cover-letters/resume-examples-for-teens

Irby, L. (2021, October 2). *10 simple ways to manage your money better*. The Balance. https://www.thebalancemoney.com/ways-to-be-better-with-money-960664

Jordan, T. (2019, January 14). *The 7 best budgeting methods*. Atypical Finance. https://www.atypicalfinance.com/7-best-budgeting-methods/

Klimashousky, D. (2019, July 23). *Making an investment plan: A step-by-step guide*. SmartAsset. https://smartasset.com/investing/how-to-make-an-investment-plan

Conclusion

Kuligowski, K. (2022, August 24). *Resume writing tips: Make your resume stand out.* Business News Daily. https://www.businessnewsdaily.com/3207-resume-writing-tips.html

MarketWatch. (2023, January 31). *Tesla inc.* MarketWatch. https://www.marketwatch.com/investing/stock/tsla

McKay, D. R. (2022, October 13). *Your step-by-step guide to choosing a career.* The Balance. https://www.thebalancemoney.com/steps-to-choosing-career-525506

Money management and budgeting tips for teens. (n.d.). Better Money Habits. https://bettermoneyhabits.bankofamerica.com/en/personal-banking/money-management-for-teens

Money Masters. (2021, November 12). *7 investing tips to become a successful investor.* Money Masters. https://moneymasters.app/blog/7-Essential-Investing-Tips

Nickolas, S. (2022, January 10). *Simple interest vs. compound interest: The main differences.* Investopedia. https://www.investopedia.com/ask/answers/042315/what-difference-between-compounding-interest-and-simple-interest.asp#:~:text=Generally%2C%20simple%20interest%20paid%20or

Nolo. (n.d.). *Money management 101.* Nolo. https://www.nolo.com/legal-encyclopedia/money-management-101-30147.html

Pelta, R. (2022, July 14). *What is career planning?* Forage. https://www.theforage.com/blog/careers/career-planning-process

Peterson, C. (2022, April 13). *Resume for teens: Examples & writing tips.* Resume Genius. https://resumegenius.com/blog/resume-help/resume-examples-for-teens

Picardo, E. (2022, July 22). *Investing explained: Types of investments and how to get started.* Investopedia. https://www.investopedia.com/terms/i/investing.asp#:~:text=P erhaps%20the%20most%20common%20are

Raising Children Network. (n.d.). *Money management for teenagers.* Raising Children Network. https://raisingchildren.net.au/pre-teens/family-life/pocket-money/money-management-for-teens

Rakoczy, C. (2022, September 29). *Helping your teen understand the costs of college.* The Balance. https://www.thebalancemoney.com/helping-your-teen-understand-the-costs-of-college-5202264

Sather, A. (2014, December 11). *5 tips of investment advice for teenagers.* Investing for Beginners. https://einvestingforbeginners.com/5-tips-investment-advice-teenagers/

Schwab Brokerage. (n.d.). *Creating an investment plan.* Schwab Brokerage. https://www.schwabmoneywise.com/essentials/creating-an-investment-plan

Schwahn, L. (2022a, May 18). *7 practical budgeting tips to help manage your money.* NerdWallet. https://www.nerdwallet.com/article/finance/budgeting-tips

Schwahn, L. (2022b, December 17). *How to choose the right budget system.* NerdWallet. https://www.nerdwallet.com/article/finance/how-to-choose-the-right-budget-system

Share, J. (2017, December 15). *Resume for teens: Writing tips to impress employers.* LiveCareer; Live Career. https://www.livecareer.com/resources/resumes/how-to/write/resume-tips-for-teenagers

Sokunbi, B. (2021, March 23). *How to spend money wisely: 5 habits to watch.* Clever Girl Finance. https://www.clevergirlfinance.com/blog/spend-money-wisely/

Conclusion

Srinivasan, H. (2022, October 1). *Your kids should start building credit early—here's how to get started.* Real Simple. https://www.realsimple.com/work-life/money/teach-kids-about-credit

Success, F. (2012, July 31). *10 practical tips from successful investors.* Brian Tracy. https://www.briantracy.com/blog/financial-success/practical-tips/

TeenVestor. (2023, January 1). *7 steps to investing as a teenager [in 2023].* TeenVestor. https://www.teenvestor.com/7steps

Town, P. (2018, April 4). *Spending money wisely: 7 ways to save more & spend less.* Rule One Investing. https://www.ruleoneinvesting.com/blog/financial-control/spending-money-wisely/

Unity College. (2021, February 9). *9 shocking tips to help you avoid student debt.* Unity College. https://unity.edu/hybrid-learning/tips-to-avoid-student-debt/

Wells Fargo. (n.d.). *What to know about the debt snowball vs avalanche method.* Wells Fargo. https://www.wellsfargo.com/goals-credit/smarter-credit/manage-your-debt/snowball-vs-avalanche-paydown/

What is a student loan? A simple explanation for kids, teens and beginners. (2020, August 4). Easy Peasy Finance for Kids and Beginners. https://www.easypeasyfinance.com/student-loans-for-kids-teens/

What is career planning? (n.d.). College for Adults. https://collegeforadults.org/career-planning/what-is-career-planning/

Yahoo Finance. (2023, January 30). *Microsoft corporation (MSFT) stock historical prices & data.* Yahoo Finance. https://finance.yahoo.com/quote/MSFT/history/?guccounter=1&guce_referrer=aHR0cHM6Ly93d3cuZ29vЗ2xlLmNvbS8&guce_referrer_sig=AQAAANy_LUvUhj-J3vsI52hhPvrCA0R0Q6RzanBGDmDX5qgF4yIsGCV4o9_hmA

Sam Peterson

FZ8PbMV9Pr988FDGLzSvYjsnjH8jQW2aYJ5ZOVqeHiKjBgU_
_80u77AnIaOnWzT-
NOKCoCHCKNRiIqWD3rh_nMBaKFHhNszVmBmxiZ5t4HS
PSSC-C3